A Complete Insulin Resistance Diet for All Ages

The Definitive Resource for Reversing Insulin Resistance While Also Controlling Obesity, Preventing Prediabetes, and Losing Weight

Dane Alfred

© Copyright 2024 - All rights reserved.

The contents of this book may not be reproduced or transmitted without written permission from the author or publisher. Under no circumstances can the publisher or author be held liable or liable for any damages, compensation, or loss of money arising from this book's information, whether directly or indirectly.

About the author

Dane Alfred was born in San Francisco in 1985. He is a dietitian and nutritionist from the USA. He graduated in Nutrition and Food Science at the University of North Carolina. Then he worked under a health specialist for 5 years. This book is part of his passion of writing and personal experiences.

Table of Contents

INTRODUCTION 7
PART 1: Understanding Insulin Resistance 8
  What is insulin resistance? 8
  Causes and Risk Factors 8
  Symptoms and Diagnosis 9
  The Link between Insulin Resistance, Obesity, and Prediabetes 10
  Getting Started with the Insulin Resistance Diet 11
  Building Your Insulin Resistance Diet 12
    Choosing the Right Foods 12
    Balancing Macronutrients 12
    Portion Control and Timing 12
    Hydration 12
    Meal Planning and Preparation 13
    Smart Snacking 13
    Reading Labels 13
    Adjusting for Individual Needs 13
PART 2: THE RECIPIES 14
  BREAKFAST 14
    1. Grilled Citrus Halibut 14
    2. Special Vegetable Stock 15
    3. Cappuccino Chocolate Chip 15
    4. Blueberry-Banana Smoothie 16
    5. Gumbo with Seafood 17
    6. Breakfast Meatloaf 17
    7. Turkey Casserole 18
    8. Waffle Sandwich 19
    9. Bagel Sandwich 19
    10. Almond-Cranberry Cereal Bar 19
    11. Chewy Date-Apple Bars 20
    12. Cherry Scones 20
    13. Omelet 21
    14. Browned Butter Mocha Latte 22
    15. Almond-Cranberry Cereal Bar 22
    16. Fried Eggs with Spinach and Mushrooms 23
    17. Greek Yogurt with Berry Bliss 24
    18. Avocado and Egg Breakfast Delight 25
    19. Spinach and Mushroom Frittata 25
    20. Smoked Salmon and Cheese Roll 26
    21. Green Smoothie 27
    22. Berry Crumble Pudding 28
    23. Chewy Date-Apple Bars 29
    24. Breakfast Meatloaf 29
    25. Mixed Veggie Omelet 30

26.	Cheesy Eggs, Bacon, and Cauliflower Hash	31
27.	Poached Salmon	31
28.	Cottage Cheese with Nut Medley	32
29.	Vegetable Korma	33
30.	Zucchini Soup	33

LUNCH 34

31.	Grilled Chicken and Avocado Salad	34
32.	Cobbler Topped with Chicken Gravy	35
33.	Deviled Egg with Pickled Jalapenos	36
34.	Herb Pesto Pork Chops	36
35.	Beef Stir-up	37
36.	Adobo Chicken	38
37.	Beef Bread	38
38.	Crispy Chicken	39
39.	Persian Chicken	40
40.	Special Noodles	41
41.	Fried Rice with Cauliflower	41
42.	Cauliflower and broccoli soup	42
43.	Stuffed Vegetables with Mushroom	43
44.	Quiche Lorraine	44
45.	Chicken Gyros	45
46.	Chicken Satay	45
47.	Pork Chops	46
48.	Chicken loaf	47
49.	Granola and Grilled Peaches	48
50.	Zesty Mediterranean Chicken Thighs	48
51.	Beef Bourguignon	49
52.	Classic Pot Roast	50
53.	Paneer Curry with Stuffed Potatoes	51
54.	Different Chicken Curry	51
55.	Rice with lentil curry	52
56.	Baked Egg	53
57.	Tuna and avocado salad	54
58.	Grilled Shrimp and Vegetable Skewers	54
59.	Lamb and pork seasoning	55
60.	Simple Chicken Gravy	56
61.	Crab Cakes with Lime Salsa	57

DINNER 58

62.	Blueberry Custard Cake in Lemon Flavor	58
63.	Rice Pudding	58
64.	Rice with Beef Gravy	59
65.	Shrimp Thermion	60
66.	Roasted Beef Stew	61
67.	Soup with Chicken and Noodles	62
68.	Beef in a Stir-Fry	62
69.	Walleye Simmered in Basil Cream	62
70.	Cheesy Tuna Casserole	63

#	Recipe	Page
71.	Ginger Beef Salad	64
72.	French Onion Soup	65
73.	Traditional Chicken-Vegetable Soup	65
74.	Grilled Chicken and Vegetable Stir-Fry	66
75.	Grilled Portobello Mushrooms with Spinach and Feta	67
76.	Zucchini Noodles with Pesto and Cherry Tomatoes	67
77.	Baked Salmon with Lemon-Dill Sauce	68
78.	Baked Chicken Thighs with Garlic and Herbs	69
79.	Eggplant Lasagna	69
80.	Spaghetti squash with pesto and cherry tomatoes	70
81.	Lemon, garlic, shrimp, and asparagus	70
82.	Stuffed bell peppers	71
83.	Grilled Cilantro Lime Chicken	71
84.	Lamb with asparagus	72
85.	Zoodles with meatballs in an Italian sauce	73
86.	Curried cauliflower soup	74
87.	Shrimp Gravy	74
88.	Cauliflower Rice and Luau Pork	75
89.	Roasted-beef Stew	76
90.	Chicken Noodle Soup	77
91.	Baked Cod with Lemon and Herbs	77
92.	Lemon Herb Grilled Chicken Breast	78
93.	Spicy Cauliflower Rice with Ground Turkey	78

SNACKS 79

#	Recipe	Page
94.	Guacamole-stuffed cucumber bites	79
95.	Caprese Skewers with a Balsamic Glaze	80
96.	Cucumber and Cream Cheese Roll-Ups	80
97.	Greek Yogurt with Berries and Almonds	81
98.	Parmesan Zucchini Crisps	81
99.	Deviled Eggs with Bacon	82
100.	Smoked Salmon with Cucumber	82
101.	Almond and Coconut Energy Bites	83
102.	Spicy Roasted Chickpeas	83
103.	Mini Bell Pepper Nachos	84
104.	Cauliflower Buffalo Bites	84
105.	Crispy Cheese	85
106.	Meatballs	85
107.	Sweet and spicy shrimp	86
108.	Cheesy spaghetti squash	86
109.	Prosciutto-Garlic Green Beans	87
110.	Fresh veggies with herbs	88
111.	Veggie Stir-Fry	88
112.	Pizza Casserole	89
113.	Sweet and spicy Thai pizza	89
114.	Pancakes	90
115.	Twist Pizza	91
116.	Diavola Pizza	92

117.	Vegan Pizza	92
118.	Grilled Sandwich	93
119.	Mini Burger Sliders	93
120.	Portobello Mushroom Burger Bites	94
121.	Tacos	95
122.	Chicken and Vegetable Kabobs	95
123.	Roasted Pepper with Chicken	96
124.	Antojitos	96

DESSERT 97

125.	Choco-Peanut Protein Bites	97
126.	Cherry Cake	97
127.	Special Cake	98
128.	Avocado Chocolate Mousse	98
129.	Berry Parfait	99
130.	Chocolate Peanut Butter Bombs	99
131.	Apple Kuchen	100
132.	Cheese Bites	100
133.	Chia Seed Pudding with Berries	101
134.	Vanilla Coconut Macaroons	101
135.	Classic Almond Chocolate Cake	102
136.	Chocolate Chip Raspberry Muffin Cake	103
137.	Decadent Dark Chocolate Almond Cake	103
138.	Zesty Lemon Custard	104
139.	Garlic Basil Cauliflower Cheese Bread	105
140.	Chocolate Cake	105
141.	Chocolate Almond Brownies	106
142.	Cheesecake	106
143.	Carrot Cake Delight	107
144.	Energy Bites	108

30-Day Meal Plan 109
Week 1 109
Week 2 110
Week 3 111
Week 4 112

CONCLUSION 113

INTRODUCTION

Insulin, a hormone essential for regulating blood sugar levels, causes the body's cells to become less sensitive. Insulin resistance is a metabolic condition that is defined by this loss of sensitivity. The accumulation of glucose in the circulation, which is the consequence of an ineffective cell response to insulin, leads to elevated blood sugar levels. Elevated insulin levels may result from the pancreas producing additional insulin as a compensatory measure over time. If left untreated, insulin resistance may progress to prediabetes or type-2 diabetes. The prevalence of this disorder in modern society is increasing due to its frequent association with obesity, sedentary lifestyles, and unhealthy eating habits. It is imperative to comprehend insulin resistance in order to prevent complications and improve one's overall health.

Food is one of the most critical components of insulin resistance treatment. Our insulin sensitivity and blood sugar levels are directly influenced by our diets. A diet that is well-balanced in macronutrients, high in whole, unprocessed foods, and low in high-GI meals is recommended to assist in the regulation of blood sugar levels and the improvement of insulin sensitivity. Diets that are rich in fiber, lean proteins, healthy lipids, and low-glycemic index carbohydrates are particularly beneficial. Two additional methods for enhancing the efficacy of nutritional measures are meal timing and portion management. The management of blood sugar levels, weight loss, prevention of obesity, and reduction in the risk of developing diabetes of any kind are all possible outcomes for those who have insulin resistance and follow a diet that is well-informed.

This book is meant to serve as a thorough manual for anybody looking to control their insulin resistance through nutrition. It provides a combination of realistic guidance, scientific explanations, and a range of age-appropriate recipes. From knowledge of insulin resistance to the science of food, meal planning, and lifestyle modifications, each chapter builds on the one before it. The book's age-specific chapters customize food suggestions to meet the particular requirements of adults, children, and older citizens. Readers may create a long-lasting and efficient strategy for controlling insulin resistance and enhancing general health by adhering to the recommendations and making use of the available resources.

PART 1: Understanding Insulin Resistance

What is insulin resistance?

There is a metabolic disease known as insulin resistance, which occurs when the cells of the body lose their sensitivity to the hormone insulin, which is produced by the pancreas and is responsible for controlling the levels of sugar in the blood.

Our bodies convert carbohydrates from food into glucose, which is subsequently discharged into the circulation. Insulin facilitates the absorption of glucose by cells, enabling them to utilize it as fuel. However, insulin resistance results in a lack of response from the cells to insulin, resulting in the retention of glucose in the bloodstream.

The body produces more insulin to make up for this decreased sensitivity, which raises the hormone's levels in the blood. At first, this could assist in maintaining normal blood sugar levels, but eventually the pancreas might find it difficult to meet the growing need for insulin. Elevated blood sugar levels and type 2-diabetes, or prediabetes, may result from this.

Numerous risk factors, including obesity, particularly extra fat around the belly, a sedentary lifestyle, a poor diet, and certain hereditary variables, are often linked to insulin resistance. Insulin resistance is also associated with diseases like metabolic syndrome and polycystic ovarian syndrome (PCOS).Insulin resistance might have mild symptoms that are often disregarded. Increasing weariness and appetite, trouble focusing, and weight gain—especially in the midsection—are typical symptoms. Sometimes black spots on the skin appear on the neck, elbows, knees, and knuckles due to insulin resistance. Insulin levels, fasting blood sugar, and sometimes an oral glucose tolerance test are used to diagnose insulin resistance. For insulin resistance to be managed and reversed with lifestyle modifications including diet, exercise, and weight reduction, early identification is essential.

Understanding insulin resistance is the initial step in accepting personal responsibility for your health.

People may lower their risk of diabetes, increase their insulin sensitivity, and improve their general well-being by being aware of the symptoms and risk factors and making educated choices.

Causes and Risk Factors

Insulin resistance is a complex condition influenced by a variety of factors, both genetic and lifestyle-related. Extra fat, especially visceral fat, which gathers in the abdominal region, is a major contributor accumulates around the abdomen. Metabolically active fats like these secrete inflammatory chemicals and fatty acids that can disrupt insulin signaling and reduce insulin sensitivity in cells.

One of the major causes of insulin resistance is a lack of physical activity . By improving metabolic health and increasing glucose uptake by muscles, regular physical exercise can increase insulin sensitivity.

Conversely, a lack of exercise can lead to weight gain and decreased muscle mass, both of which are linked to insulin resistance.

Additionally, the diet is of crucial importance. Insulin resistance can be exacerbated by diets that are excessively high in refined carbohydrates, sugary foods, and harmful lipids. These foods can result in abrupt increases in blood sugar and insulin levels, which can contribute to increased fat storage and inflammation. The problem can be further exacerbated by a diet that is deficient in fiber, lean proteins, and healthy lipids, as it fails to supply the optimal nutrients for metabolic function.

The genetic makeup of a person may also play a role in the development of insulin resistance. There is a correlation between having a family history of metabolic syndrome or type 2-diabetes and an increased likelihood of getting the given ailment. In addition, particular racial and ethnic groups, including African Americans, Hispanics, Native Americans, and Asians, are at a higher risk than other groups. Other factors include age and hormonal changes. As people age, they naturally become more prone to insulin resistance. Polycystic ovarian syndrome (PCOS) and other hormonal disorders might impact insulin sensitivity as well.

Poor sleep and chronic stress are additional risk factors. Blood sugar levels and insulin production can be elevated by stress hormones such as cortical. The balance of hormones that regulate hunger and appetite is disrupted by inadequate sleep, which may result in insulin resistance and weight gain. It is imperative to comprehend these causes and risk factors in order to prevent and manage insulin resistance. Individuals can substantially reduce their risk and enhance their overall health by addressing lifestyle factors and making informed choices.

Symptoms and Diagnosis

Insulin resistance might appear initially with no symptoms and frequently develop gradually. But when the illness worsens, certain symptoms and indicators could show up. Polyphagia, or excessive hunger, is a typical sign of poor cell absorption of glucose, which causes the body to seek more food. Overeating and consequent weight gain, especially around the belly, may result from this.

Weakness is yet another common symptom. Insulin-resistant people may experience exceptional fatigue and sluggishness even after a full night's sleep because their cells are not getting enough glucose, the body's main energy source. The daily routine and general quality of life may be impacted by this lack of energy.

Accomplishing focus is another sign of insulin resistance, which is also known as "brain fog." The brain's inability to get enough glucose, which is necessary for optimum performance, is the cause of this cognitive impairment. Insulin resistance sometimes brings on blood sugar fluctuations might also cause irritation or mood changes in some individuals. Acanthosis Nigerians, a disorder characterized by darker skin patches. These patches often show up on the knuckles, elbows, knees, armpits, and neck. These regions may also see the development of skin tags, which are tiny growths of skin.

Healthcare professionals usually start with a complete medical history and a physical examination to detect insulin resistance. Fasting insulin and blood glucose levels are often measured as part of blood tests, which are essential for diagnosis. An elevated level of fasting insulin may suggest that the pancreas is generating more insulin to make up for decreased sensitivity. An extra diagnostic procedure is the oral glucose tolerance test (OGTT).

A glucose-rich drink is consumed throughout the test, and the subject's blood sugar is then periodically checked. Insulin resistance may be demonstrated during the test by elevated blood sugar levels.

Additionally, the hemoglobin A1C test, which finds the mean blood glucose levels from the past 2-3 months, could be used.

While it is frequently employed to diagnose diabetes, it may also offer insights into potential insulin resistance and long-term blood sugar regulation.

Effective management of insulin resistance requires an early diagnosis. Through early detection of symptoms and proper testing, people may increase their insulin sensitivity and stop the disease from becoming worse and becoming type 2 diabetic.

The Link between Insulin Resistance, Obesity, and Prediabetes

Understanding the relationship among obesity, prediabetes, and insulin resistance is essential to comprehending metabolic health. Insulin resistance is often the common denominator across these disorders, starting a vicious cycle that, if left unchecked, might result in more serious health problems.

There is a strong correlation between obesity and insulin resistance, especially abdominal obesity. Extra body fat, particularly the visceral fat around the organs, produces a number of bioactive compounds that disrupt insulin signaling, including inflammatory cytokines and free fatty acids. Because of this interference, glucose cannot enter cells as effectively, and the pancreas must create more insulin to make up for it. Chronically elevated insulin levels have the potential to worsen insulin resistance over time, starting a vicious cycle. Insulin resistance is a critical phase in the progression to prediabetes. Prediabetes is characterized by blood sugar levels that are elevated but not elevated enough to be classified as type-2 diabetes. This illness implies that the body is experiencing difficulty in effectively regulating glucose. Insulin resistance is a critical element of prediabetes, a condition in which the body's need for insulin to regulate blood sugar levels increases as a result of the cells' inability to respond to insulin. If type 2diabetes is not treated, prediabetes may progress to diabetes, which poses a variety of health risks, such as renal complications, neurological damage, and cardiovascular disease.

Furthermore, the management of weight becomes challenging when obesity and insulin resistance are present. Insulin resistance may complicate weight loss efforts due to the fact that elevated insulin levels promote fat accumulation and increase appetite. Obesity and insulin resistance are perpetuated by the challenges associated with weight loss.

In order to address this interconnected trio, a comprehensive strategy emphasizing dietary, exercise, and lifestyle modifications are needed. Crucial components include a healthy diet low in processed foods and added sugars, frequent exercise, including strength and aerobic training, techniques for stress management, and better sleep. People may end the cycle, increase their sensitivity to insulin, and lower their chance of developing type-2 diabetes by focusing on these areas. For successful preventive and treatment methods, it is essential to comprehend the relationships that exist between obesity, prediabetes, and insulin resistance.

Getting Started with the Insulin Resistance Diet

Starting an insulin resistance diet is a proactive way to enhance your well-being and stop insulin resistance from developing into more serious diseases like type-2 diabetes. Evaluating your present eating habits is the first step towards getting started. Observe what you eat, when you eat, and how much you consume. Setting reasonable dietary goals and recognizing areas that need modification require this self-awareness.

Establishing a regular schedule for eating is crucial.

Consuming meals that are nutritionally sound and include a wide range of nutrients is something that should be done consistently. Make the eating of whole, unprocessed foods a top priority. Vegetables, fruits, lean meats, entire grains, and other good fats are a few examples.

Both the management of blood sugar levels and the improvement of insulin sensitivity are associated with the consumption of certain dietary components. It is essential to refrain from consuming refined sugars and carbohydrates, as they have the potential to rapidly elevate blood glucose and insulin levels. Instead, opt for complex carbohydrates, as they are digested at a slower pace and provide consistent energy.

Part control is still another important factor. Large meals have been linked to elevated insulin production and blood sugar levels. Maintaining steady blood sugar levels all day long may require eating smaller, more frequent meals.

Additionally, this approach may assist in regulating appetite and preventing overindulgence.

Drinking enough water is also essential. Water consumption promotes healthy digestion and helps the body operate at its best. Steer clear of sugar-filled beverages since they may exacerbate insulin resistance and cause weight gain.

Make sure to thoroughly read the labels when you go grocery shopping. Choose products that are low in added sugars and high in fiber.

The best options are usually fresh, whole foods, but if you choose packaged goods, choose ones with easily identifiable, basic components.

Adding regular exercise to your schedule will enhance the dietary adjustments. Exercise assists in managing weight and enhances insulin sensitivity. Combine cardiovascular exercises like running or cycling with strength training like lifting weights or using resistance bands.

In conclusion, it is essential that you monitor your progress.

Maintain a record of your meals, exercise, and any changes to your weight or emotional state. Maintaining your motivation and implementing the necessary food and lifestyle modifications may be helped by this.

Building Your Insulin Resistance Diet

A balanced macronutrient intake, thoughtful eating practices, and well-planned food selections are all necessary to create a successful insulin resistance diet. Improving insulin sensitivity, controlling blood sugar, and promoting general health are the objectives.

Choosing the Right Foods

Emphasize whole, unprocessed foods. You should eat a diet high in vegetables, especially non-starchy ones like broccoli, peppers, and leafy greens. They are nutrient dense, low in calories, and high in fiber.

Fruits are also good for you, but focus on the lower-GI fruits like pears, apples, and berries. Whole grains are superior to refined grains.

Whole wheat, quinoa, brown rice, oats, and other high-fiber foods provide a steady energy boost. Legumes, such as beans, lentils, and chickpeas, are abundant in protein and beneficial fiber.

Include plant-based proteins like tofu and tempeh as well as lean proteins like fish, poultry, and turkey. These maintain your sense of fullness and help normalize blood sugar levels.

Healthy fats, which are present in foods such as avocados, almonds, seeds, and vegetable oil, are also crucial.

These fats help strengthen heart health and increase insulin sensitivity.

Balancing Macronutrients

A healthy mix of fats, proteins, and carbs should be included in each meal. Half of your plate should be made up of non-starchy veggies, 25% should be made up of lean protein, and the remaining 25% should be made up of healthy grains or starchy vegetables. This equilibrium promotes steady energy levels throughout the day and helps to regulate blood sugar levels.

Portion Control and Timing

Portion control is the primary strategy for managing insulin resistance. Consider the quantity of the servings and opt for smaller dishes. In addition to preventing excess, consuming smaller, more frequent meals may assist in maintaining consistent blood sugar levels. Attempt to consume food every 3.4–7 hours, and if necessary, incorporate nutritious treats.

Hydration

Staying well-hydrated is vital. For optimal digestion and glucose regulation, water is the way to go.

Refrain from consuming saccharine beverages, such as soda and sweetened liquids, as they can induce rapid blood sugar fluctuations and exacerbate insulin resistance.

Meal Planning and Preparation

Preparing your meals in advance can assist you in making healthier decisions and avoiding last-minute harmful alternatives. To maintain control over the ingredients and portion proportions, it is recommended that meals be prepared at home to the greatest extent feasible. You can ensure that you have nutritious dishes ready to go and save time by batch cooking and meal prepping.

Smart Snacking

Choose snacks that combine protein, fiber, and healthy fats to keep you satisfied between meals. Good options include a handful of nuts, Greek yogurt with berries, hummus with vegetable sticks, or an apple with almond butter. These meals can help curb hunger pangs and keep blood sugar levels in check.

Reading Labels

Always carefully read the labels when purchasing packaged items. Seek products with minimally processed components, high fiber content, and low added sugar content. You can support your insulin-resistant diet by making educated decisions by being aware of the information on nutrition labels.

Adjusting for Individual Needs

Everyone's body responds differently to dietary changes, so it's important to adjust your diet based on how you feel and any medical advice you receive. Monitor your blood sugar levels if necessary, and make adjustments to your diet to maintain optimal health.

Building an insulin-resistant diet is a dynamic process that requires attention to food choices, portion sizes, and meal timing. By focusing on whole, nutrient-dense foods, balancing macronutrients, staying hydrated and planning ahead, you can create a diet that enhances insulin sensitivity, manages blood sugar levels, and supports overall well-being.

PART 2: THE RECIPIES
BREAKFAST

1. Grilled Citrus Halibut

What we need:
- 2 really large navel oranges, each on its own
- 2 teaspoons of sharp lemon juice
- 1 tablespoon of snipped fresh mint leaves
- 1 teaspoon of vegetable oil
- 2 tablespoons of ground ginger that has been toasted
- 1 milligram of honey in a teaspoon
- ¼ teaspoon salt
- ¼ milligram of black pepper that has been organically ground
- 4 halibut fillets, skinless, weighing about 114 pounds
- The spray of cooking
- Sprigs of mint, if desired (optional)

Getting ready:
1. Bring the temperature of the flame broiler up to medium-high.
2. Cut a hole in the middle of an orange.
3. Make a total of eight slices from the remaining orange.
4. On a very large bowl, combine the lemon juice with the following six items on the list. Include fish and orange slices, and then gently toss to cover everything.
5. Place the fish and orange slices on a rack that has been coated with a cooking splash before placing it in the broiler.
6. Discard the lemon mixture. Place orange sections, chop-side down, on the rack that is in the flame broiler.
7. Flame the broiler awaiting the salmon flake easily while tested with a branch. After some minutes, flip the fish over and make orange incisions in it.
8. Place two orange slices on top of each one. Crush the orange sections and distribute them evenly over the fish and orange slices. In the event that it is desired, garnish with sprigs of mint.

2. Special Vegetable Stock

What we need:
- 4 quarts of ice-cold water that has been filtered
- ½ whole peppercorns (peppercorns)
- Three carrots, peeled and sliced, for garnish
- Three celery stalks, diced and in a bowl.
- Two bay leaves in the bud
- Four cloves of garlic that have been crushed
- One big quartered onion
- Two teaspoons of vinegar made from apple cider
- Any and any remaining veggie leftovers

Getting ready:
1. Set all of the elements inside of your slow cooker and cover up it.
2. Do not turn it on, and give it a chance to sit for half an hour.
3. Once it is finished, place it in the microwave and steam it on low for 12 hours.
4. The solids should be discarded once the broth has been strained.
5. Before using, let the stock sit in the fridge for at least 2-3 hours.
6. The freshness of stock may be preserved in the refrigerator for three to four days, or it can be kept frozen permanently.

3. Cappuccino Chocolate Chip

What we need:
- Cooking shower
- 1 and 3/4 cups low-fat heating blend
- Sugar (½ cup)
- ½ cup high-temperature water
- 2 tablespoons moment coffee granules
- Canola oil (¼ cup)
- One enormous egg
- Half a cup of semisweet chocolate is smaller than regular chips.

Getting ready:
1. Preheat the broiler to 400°.
2. Put 12 paper biscuit cup liner in the biscuit cups; cover them with cooking mist.
3. Put the mixture into dry measuring cups, being careful to keep the cups level with the blade. Whisk the heating mixture and sugar together in a medium bowl.
4. Join ½ cup of high-temperature water and espresso granules, blending until espresso breaks down. Consolidate the oil and egg, mixing with a whisk; mix in an espresso

blend. Add espresso blend to the heating blend, mixing just until sodden. Blend in chocolate-scaled-down chips.

5. Spoon the player into arranged liners. Heat it for 20 minutes at 400°F so that the biscuits spring back when contacted softly. Expel the biscuits from the container quickly and put them on a line rack. Serve warm.

4. Blueberry-Banana Smoothie

What we need:
- 1 ripe banana
- ½ cup fresh blueberries
- 1 ½ tablespoon honey
- ½ cup almond milk
- ½ teaspoon pure vanilla essence
- ½ cup Greek yogurt
- Ice cubes as your desire

Getting ready:

1. Skin the banana and put it in the blender.

Place the fresh or frozen blueberries into the blender. You may make your smoothie thicker and frothier by adding frozen blueberries.

2. Spoon the yogurt. It increases protein boost and creaminess to your smoothie.
3. Add the almond milk to the blender. Adjust the quantity to achieve your preferred thickness. If you desire extra sweetness, drizzle in the honey. You can regulate the amount based on your flavor preference and the natural sweetness of your ingredients.

Enhance the flavor with pure vanilla essence. It adds a delightful depth to your smoothie. Add some ice cubes for a thicker and colder smoothie if you like.

4. Secure the blender lid, and mix all the elements until smooth. If the mixture is too pulpy, add more almond milk to reach your desired consistency.
5. Before serving, give your banana-blueberry smoothie a quick taste test. Adjust the sweetness or thickness as needed by adding honey or milk.
6. Pour your refreshing banana-blueberry smoothie into a glass or travel cup. It's perfect for breakfast, a post-workout recovery, or a nutritious snack to satisfy your sweet cravings while keeping it healthy.

5. Gumbo with Seafood

What we need:
- 20 ounces of okra that has been frozen and then thawed
- 1 pound of skinless and boneless chicken thighs that have been pieces
- 10-ounces of shrimp after being cooked
- A chicken broth equivalent to 2 cups
- Cayenne pepper, measured up to be a half teaspoon
- 2 cups of tomato sauce with no added sugar
- 2 celery stalks, diced, are included.
- 1 ½ cups of thinly sliced onions
- 2 diced and sausages
- 2 bay leaves in the bud
- 1 ½ cups of green bell peppers that have been seeded and sliced
- As required, pepper and salt may be used.
- 3 cloves of garlic that have been smashed
- ½ of a teaspoon of dried onion flakes
- A Pinch of Zatarain's Original Gumbo File, Pure Ground

Getting ready:
1. In the cooker, mix all of the ingredients, with the exception of the shrimp and Zatarain's.
2. Within close proximity to the lid of the pan.
3. The process of cooking at a low temperature for six to eight hours
4. Then, ten minutes before the end of the time allotment, swirl it into your shrimp that has already been precooked.
5. At the time of serving the dish, shake over some Zatarain's over it.
6. Serve with rice made from cauliflower.

6. Breakfast Meatloaf

What we need:
- One pound of ground pork
- One tsp. paprika
- Two eggs
- 2 cups chopped onion
- ½ cup almond flour
- One tablespoon of coconut oil
- One tablespoon of garlic paste
- One pound of ground turkey

- Six teaspoons of Italian seasoning
- Two teaspoons of red pepper flakes
- Use salt and pepper.

Getting ready:
1. Pour oil into a pan and heat it up at a low-medium temperature.
2. When warm, mix the onion and heat it up until it is transparent.
3. Take away it from the heat.
4. Add almond flour, eggs, and seasonings to a dish and stir.
5. Add meat as well as onions, and then combine using clean hands. Shape into a loaf.
6. Grease the cooker with a coconut-oil.
7. Put the loaf in your slow cooker, making sure there's at least a half-inch space between the meat and the sides of the cooker and that the top of the loaf is flat.
8. Adjacent to the cover of the pan.
9. Heat on high for 180 minutes, so that the meat reaches 150 degrees.
10. If you want the loaf to be substantial and not crumbly, let it sit in the cooker for 15–30 minutes after cooking, with the cooker turned off and the lid removed.
11. Eat!

7. Turkey Casserole

What we need:
- Ten fresh eggs
- ½-ounce turkey sausage
- One mug of no-sugar-added salsa
- One mug of heavy cream
- Salt and pepper
- One mug of Mexican cheese blended
- One teaspoon of chili flexes
- Half teaspoon of garlic paste
- ½ tsp. cumin

Getting ready:
1. Heat a skillet and cook the sausage.
2. When it isn't pink, blend in salsa and seasonings.
3. Put out from warmth.
4. Take a dish, beat the eggs and milk as needed.
5. Mix the pork as well as the cheese, and stir.
6. Prepare a crock-pot with a coconut-oil-based cooking spray.
7. Pour in the casserole and close the cover.

8. Heat on low for five hours, or if you want to eat sooner, on high for 2–12 hours.

8. Waffle Sandwich

What we need:
- 1 (1.33-ounce) solidified multigrain waffle
- 2 tablespoons cream cheese, mollified
- 2 teaspoons dark-colored sugar
- Ground cinnamon (¼ teaspoon)
- 1 tablespoon raisins
- 1 tablespoon hacked pecans, toasted

Getting ready:
1. Toast waffles as per bundle headings.
2. Blend cream cheese, dark sugar, and cinnamon until very well mixed. Spread cream cheese blend over waffles. Sprinkle with raisins and pecans.
3. Cut the waffle down the middle. Sandwich waffle parts together with filling inside.

9. Bagel Sandwich

What we need:
- ½ cup (4 ounces) goat cheddar, disintegrated
- 4 ounces cheese cream mollified
- 1 tablespoons of honey
- 1/3 cup hacked toasted pecans
- 1 cinnamon-raisin twirl small bagel, split and toasted
- ¼ cup red Anjou pear, unpeeled and meagerly cut

Getting ready:
1. Consolidate the initial three ingredients in a little bowl. Mix in pecans.
2. Spread 1 tablespoon goat cheddar uniformly onto the cut sides of the bagel.
3. Spot pear cuts on the base portion of the bagel. Supplant the bagel top.
4. Spread and chill, staying spread as long as a multi-week.

10. Almond-Cranberry Cereal Bar

What we need:
- Almond margarine (½ cup)
- Sugar (2/3 cup)
- 5 cups of fresh wheat grain squares
- Dried cranberries (3/4 cup)

- ½ cup fragmented almonds, toasted
- Cooking shower

Getting ready:
1. Spoon almond margarine and honey into a large Dutch broiler. Boil on medium heat. Blend with oats, cranberries, and almonds, hurling to coat.
2. Put the blend into a prepared dish covered with a cooking splash, squeezing it into an even layer with cling wrap.
3. Let stand 1 hour so that set. Cut into 12 bars.

11. Chewy Date-Apple Bars

What we need:
- Two and a half cups for the entire set of dates
- 1 cup of dried apples
- ½ cup Pecans, toasted
- ½ cup Rolled oats
- ¼ teaspoon Ground cinnamon

Getting ready:
1. Bring the oven down to 350 degrees.
2. Put the initial three ingredients into a blender and mix until the leafy foods are finely slashed.
3. Include oats and cinnamon; beat 8 to multiple times so that soggy and oats are cleaved. Blend into a delicately lubed 9 x 5-inch portion container, squeezing into an even layer with a saran cover.
4. Heat for 15 minutes at 350°F. Cool completely in a dish on a line rack. Then cut into 12 bars.

12. Cherry Scones

What we need:
- 9 ounces of flour (around 2 cups)
- Salt
- Sugar (¼ cup)
- Heating powder (One and a half teaspoon)
- ¼ cup chilled, unsalted margarine
- 3/4 cup dried tart fruits, slashed
- Fat free buttermilk (3/4 cup)
- Cooking shower
- 1 tablespoon turbaned sugar (discretionary)

Getting ready:
1. Bring the oven down to 425°.
2. Estimate or softly spoon flour within dry estimating cups; then, smooth with a blade.
3. Consolidate the salt, powder, flour, and sugar in a big dish, combination admirably with a whisker. Then cut in the spread, utilizing a baked good blender, until the blend looks like coarse supper. Blend in fruits.
4. Include buttermilk and almonds separately whenever wanted, mixing just until damp.
5. Mix the butter onto a daintily floured exterior and massage lightly multiple times, including with floured hands. Structure the mixture in an 8-inch saucepan on a prepared sheet covered with a parchment pepper.
6. Cut the butter into 10 wedges, slicing into but not through the combination. Coat the top of the butter with cooking spray. Sprinkle with turbinate sugar whenever desired.
7. Keep the preparation sheet on a rack on the stove. Heat it at 425° for 20 minutes so that brilliant.

13. Omelet

What we need:
- 1 tablespoon in addition to 1 teaspoon ghee or unsalted margarine, separated
- ¼ cup diced onions
- 14 cup cut mushrooms
- 2 tablespoons diced green or red ringer peppers
- ¼ teaspoon acceptable ocean salt, partitioned
- 4 enormous eggs, beaten
- ¼ cup destroyed sharp cheddar, in addition to extra for topping sliced green onions, for trimming
- ¼ cup salsa, for serving
- 1 cup acrid cream, for serving

Getting ready:
1. Liquefy 1 tablespoon ghee in a cooker approximately low- medium heat. Include the onions, mushrooms, and ringer peppers and cook, blending, so that the onions and peppers are delicate. The mushrooms are brilliant. Include the ground meat and fry until cooked from side to side, around 3 minutes. Then, flavor with 1/8 teaspoon salt.
2. Use a blending bowl, beat the eggs, water, and the remaining salt and mix well. Put it in a safe spot.
3. Heat a 12-inch pan at a medium-low temperature. Include the rest of the teaspoon of ghee and swirl to coat the dish. Empty the egg into the blender. Spread and cook until the eggs are nearly set. Evacuate the top and sprinkle in the cheddar to cover the whole omelet. Spoon the vegetable filling over the cheddar.

4. Crease the omelet down the middle and serve on a plate. Dust with extra cheddar and onions. Present with the acrid cream and salsa.
5. Store additional items in a sealed holder in the icebox for as long as 3 days. Heat before taking!

14. Browned Butter Mocha Latte

What we need:
- Unsalted butter (2 tablespoons)
- 1 1/4 cups unsweetened cashew milk (or hemp milk if sans nuts)
- 2 tablespoons unsweetened cocoa powder, in addition to extra for topping (discretionary)
- 2 tablespoons of powdered sugar
- 3 tablespoons hot fermented decaf coffee or other solid blended decaf espresso, Whipped cream, for trimming (discretionary)
- Special equipment (discretionary)
- Immersion blender

Getting ready:
1. Pour the butter in a cooker approximately high heat, mixing until the butter froths and dark-colored spots start to show up around 5 minutes; this is browned butter. If utilizing butter-seasoned coconut oil, heat the oil just until softened.
2. Decrease the warmth to medium and gradually rush in the cashew milk; it will sizzle as you add it to the browned butter. Stir the cocoa powder and sugar. Whenever wanted, embed an infusion blender and mix until the blend takes the shape of a foamy latte, around 1 minute.
3. Empty the coffee into a giant cup. Include the hot milk blend and mix well. Serve promptly, decorated with whipped cream and a sprinkle of unsweetened cocoa powder, whenever wanted.

15. Almond-Cranberry Cereal Bar

What we need:
- ½ cup Almond margarine
- 2 cup Honey
- 5 cups of fresh wheat grain squares
- Dried cranberries (3/4 cup)
- ½ cup fragmented almonds, toasted
- Cooking shower

Getting ready:
1. Spoon almond margarine and honey into a large Dutch broiler. Boil on medium heat. Blend with oats, cranberries, and almonds, hurling to coat.

2. Put the blend into a prepared dish covered with a cooking splash, squeezing it into an even layer with cling wrap.
3. Let stand 1 hour so that set. Cut into 12 bars.

16. Fried Eggs with Spinach and Mushrooms

What we need:
- 6 jumbo sized eggs
- 2 teaspoons of vegetable oil
- 4 garlic minced cloves
- 1 cup of chopped fresh spinach, measuring cup
- Grated mozzarella cheese equaling one-half cup
- 1 cup of mushrooms, cut into thin slices
- ½ of an onion cut very small
- Various amounts of salt & pepper, to taste
- To finish, sprinkle with some fresh herbs, such parsley or chives.

Getting ready:
1. Vegetable oil should be greased on heated oven to medium heat in an ovenproof pan, ideally one that does not stick. After approximately two to three minutes, add the diced onions and crushed garlic then continue cooking once they become clear and the garlic smells good.
2. The sliced mushrooms should be added to the pan and given a further three to four minutes of cooking time, so that they begin to brown and lose their moisture.

Add the chopped spinach and continue to fry for another one to two minutes so that the spinach has sagging and any extra moisture has evaporated, whichever comes first. Before combining, season with salt and pepper to taste.

3. Take a separate dish; give the eggs a good whisking all the way through. Combine the grated cheese with the rest of the ingredients.

The egg and cheese mixture should be poured over the veggies that have been sautéed in the pan. Carefully mix the ingredients until they are evenly distributed.

4. On the burner, let the frittata to cook undisturbed for three to four minutes, which will enable the edges to firm.
5. After the oven has been prepared, place the pan inside and bake the frittata for around fifteen to twenty minutes, so that the middle is completely set and the frittata has puffed up. You may determine whether or not anything is cooked through by putting a knife or toothpick into the middle and seeing whether or not it emerges uncontaminated.
6. After the food has finished cooking, take the skillet out of the oven. Before slicing it into wedges, let it come to room temperature first.

7. Add a splash of flavor and color to your frittata by topping it with fresh herbs, such as chopped parsley or chives. This will give the dish a nice finishing touch.
8. Serve the frittata hot as a filling breakfast, a light and protein-packed lunch or supper, or even as a snack in between meals. I hope you like your handmade frittata with spinach and mushrooms!

17. Greek Yogurt with Berry Bliss

What we need:
- ½ cup mixed berries
- 1 tablespoon honey to taste
- 1 cup Greek yogurt
- 1 tablespoon of crushed nuts

Getting ready:
1. Wash and gently pat dry the fresh berries. If you're using strawberries, remove the green tops and slice them for mixing.
2. Take a mixing bowl, add the Greek yogurt. If you desire a touch of sweetness, add the honey over the yogurt.
3. If you want to enhance the flavor of your yogurt, add a few drops of pure vanilla essence. This step is entirely optional but can add a delightful depth of flavor.
4. By a spoon to gently wrinkle the honey into the Greek yogurt awaiting the mixture is sweetener and the silky is evenly distributed. Taste and adjust the sweetness if needed.
5. In a serving glass or bowl, start by spooning a layer of sweetened Greek yogurt. Layer on top of that some fresh berries. Repeat the process until you've used up all your ingredients. Top it off with an extra berry or two for a burst of color.
6. Alternatively, mix the fresh berries directly into the sweetened Greek yogurt for a vibrant, berry-infused yogurt.
7. For a textural contrast and added richness, shake over some diced nuts on apex of your Greek yogurt and berry creation.
8. Your Greek Yogurt with Berry Bliss is ready to savor. Whether you chose layers or a mixed medley, each spoonful combines the creamy tanginess of Greek yogurt with the usual attractiveness and juiciness of fresh berries. The touch of honey and optional nuts add layers of flavor and texture that make this simple yet elegant dish a delightful treat.
9. Feel free to get creative with your Greek yogurt and berry concoction. Experiment with different berries, drizzles (try maple syrup for a different twist), or additional toppings like granola for extra crunch.

18. Avocado and Egg Breakfast Delight

What we need:
- 1 ripe avocado
- 2 large eggs
- Pepper and Salt to taste
- Fresh herbs like chives, parsley
- Hot sauce or salsa (optional, for added kick)

Getting ready:
1. Begin by preheating your oven. This will ensure your avocado and eggs cook evenly. Cut the ripe avocado. To create a stable base, you may need to slice a small portion of the rounded side of each avocado half.
2. Carefully scoop out some of the flesh from each avocado half to create a small hollow that can accommodate an egg. Reserve the scooped-out avocado for later use in salads or spreads.
3. Season both halves of the avocado with a little salt and pepper. Add some flavor to your cuisine with this easy spice. Gently crack one large egg into each avocado half. Be mindful not to overflow the hollow—adjust the amount of egg whites if needed to fit comfortably within the avocado.
4. Add another pinch of pepper and salt on top of the eggs for seasoning. If you enjoy a bit of heat, a dash of hot sauce or a spoonful of salsa can be a delightful addition at this stage.
5. Place the stuffed avocado halves on a baking sheet or oven-safe dish. Transfer them with caution to the oven that has been prepared. Cook for around ½ to fifteen minutes, depending on your oven, so that the whites of egg set while the yolks remain faintly runny. If you prefer your eggs well-done, bake for an additional few minutes.
6. Once out of the oven, garnish your avocado and egg creations with fresh herbs like chopped chives or parsley. These not only attach a burst of color other than also an extra layer of freshness.
7. Serve your avocado and egg breakfast delight hot and savor the creamy richness of the avocado blending with the lusciousness of the perfectly baked eggs.

19. Spinach and Mushroom Frittata

What we need:
- 3 tablespoons of vegetable oil
- 3 cloves diced garlic
- 1 cup minced spinach
- 7 large eggs
- ½ cup mozzarella cheese

- ½ finely chopped onion
- 1 cup sliced mushrooms
- Pepper and Salt, to taste
- Herbs parsley or chives

Getting ready:

1. Prepare your oven by preheating it. In a pan that can be placed in the oven, vegetable oil should be warmed up over a low temperature. Ideally, the pan should be one that does not stick. After around two to three minutes, mix the garlic minced and diced onion, and continues to sauté them till they turn brown and aromatic.
2. Mix the sliced mushrooms and sliced spinach to the cooker and fry for three to four minutes more so that they begin to brown and release their moisture.
3. Flavor the vegetable pepper with and salt as your taste. Beat all eggs in a mixing dish place to one side them. Stir in the grated Parmesan cheese.
4. After the veggies have been sautéed, layer the beaten egg and mozzarella mixture on top of them in pan. Smoothly swirl to mix the ingredients evenly. Let the frittata cook undisturbed for 3–4 minutes on the stovetop, allowing the top to set.
5. After the oven has been warmed, place the pan inside and bake the frittata for roughly fifteen to twenty minutes, until it has puffed up and the middle is fully set.
6. Once cooked, take away the skillet out of the oven (remember to use oven mitts, as the handle will be hot). Allow it to cool slightly before slicing into wedges. Garnish your spinach and mushroom frittata with minced chives.
7. Enjoy.

20. Smoked Salmon and Cheese Roll

What we need:
- 4 ounces smoked salmon slices
- 4 ounces cream cheese, softened
- ½ cucumber, thinly chopped into strips
- Fresh dill sprigs
- Lemon zest (optional, for extra freshness)
- Freshly ground black pepper (optional, for added flavor)

Getting ready:

1. Start by laying out your smoked salmon slices, ensuring they are dry. For easier spreading, let the cream cheese soften at room temperature . Thinly slice the cucumber into strips, and gather fresh dill sprigs for garnish.
2. Take a piece of smoked salmon and gently extend a coat of softened cheese cream above it. The amount of cream cheese you use may vary based on personal preference, but a thin, even layer works well.

3. Place a few thin cucumber strips horizontally at one end of the salmon slice. These will give every roll-up an exciting burst of flavor and texture.
4. Carefully roll up the smoked salmon slice with the cream cheese and cucumber inside. Squeeze out as much filler as possible while rolling it tightly.
5. Repeat the process with the remaining smoked salmon slices, cream cheese, and cucumber strips.
6. Using a sharp knife, slice each rolled-up salmon into bite-sized pieces. Garnish with fresh dill sprigs for an extra splash of color and zest. You can also zest some lemon over the roll-ups for an extra layer of flavor.
7. Arrange your smoked salmon and cream cheese roll-ups on a platter or serving dish. They're ready to serve as an elegant appetizer or a light and flavorful snack.

21. Green Smoothie

What we need:
- 1 cup unsweetened almond milk
- 1 scoop of your favorite protein powder
- ½ ripe avocados
- 1 cup of fresh spinach leaves
- 1 tablespoon almond butter (unsweetened)
- ½ teaspoon vanilla essence
- Ice cubes (optional, for desired thickness)
- Sweetener (optional, to taste; use a sugar substitute like stevia or erythritol)

Getting ready:
1. For a smoother blending experience, you can use pre-chilled almond milk or add ice cubes. Add the unsweetened almond milk to your blender as the base.
2. Toss in the fresh spinach leaves. Your smoothie will get a healthy dose of color and nutrients from these nutrient-dense greens. Scoop out the ripe avocado and add it to the blender. Creaminess and healthful fats are both contributed by avocado.
3. Incorporate a scoop of your chosen protein powder. This adds essential protein to your smoothie, keeping you fuller for longer. Spoon the almond butter. It adds a delightful nutty flavor and an extra dose of healthy fats and protein.
4. Pure vanilla essence elevates the taste profile. A small amount goes a long way in making your smoothie taste sweeter without added sugar. Depending on your preference, you can adjust the sweetness by adding stevia or erythritol . Keep in mind that the ripe avocado and protein powder might already provide some sweetness.
5. Secure the blender lid, and combine everything waiting creamy and smooth. You can adjust the thickness by addition ice cubes, if desired.

6. Check the sweetness and thickness of your green smoothie with a sip before serving. If you like a thinner Transfer your healthy green smoothie to a glass or a portable cup. It's perfect for a quick breakfast on busy mornings, a post-workout refuel, or a healthy snack any time of the day.

22. Berry Crumble Pudding

What we need:
For the filling:
- 4 cups mixed berries
- ¼ cup honey
- vanilla extract 1 teaspoon
- lemon juice 1 tablespoon
- 1 tablespoon almond flour (to thicken)

For the topping:
- ½ cup unsweetened shredded coconut
- 1 cup of almond flour
- ½ cup chopped nuts
- ¼ cup granulated erythritol or your preferred sweetener
- ½ teaspoon cinnamon
- 1/4 teaspoon salt
- ½ cup butter
- 1 teaspoon of vanilla essence

Getting ready:
1. Almond flour, lemon juice, vanilla essence, granulated erythritol, and mixed berries should all be combined in a big mixing basin. To evenly coat the berries, gently stir.
2. Transfer the berry mixture to a greased baking dish, spreading it out evenly.
3. In a separate bowl, whisk together the almond flour, almonds, granulated erythritol, salt, cinnamon, and unsweetened shredded coconut.
4. Mix the dry ingredients with the melted butter or coconut oil and vanilla essence. Mix until the dough is crumbly and fully mixed.
5. Over the berry mixture in the baking dish, evenly distribute the crumble topping.
6. After preheating the oven, place the baking dish inside and bake for 25 to 30 minutes, or until the berries are bubbling and the topping is golden brown.
7. Remove the berry crumble pudding from the oven and let it cool slightly before serving.

23. Chewy Date-Apple Bars

What we need:
- Two and a half cups for the entire set of dates
- 1 cup of dried apples
- Pecans, toasted (½ cup)
- Rolled oats (½ cup)
- Ground cinnamon (¼ teaspoon)

Getting ready:
1. Bring the microwave down to preheat.
2. Put the initial three ingredients into a blender and mix until the leafy foods are finely slashed.
3. Include oats and cinnamon; beat 8 to multiple times so that soggy and oats are cleaved. Blend into a delicately lubed 9 x 5-inch portion container, squeezing into an even layer with a saran cover.
4. Heat for 15 minutes at 350°F. Cool completely in a dish on a line rack. Then cut into 12 bars.

24. Breakfast Meatloaf

What we need:
- One pound of ground pork
- One teaspoon of paprika
- Two eggs
- 2 cups chopped onion
- ½ cup almond flour
- One tablespoon of coconut oil
- One tablespoon of garlic paste
- One pound of ground turkey
- Six teaspoons of Italian seasoning
- Two teaspoons of red pepper flakes
- Use salt and pepper.

Getting ready:
1. Pour oil into a pan and heat it up to a low-medium temperature.
2. When warm, mix the onion and heat it up until it is transparent.
3. Take it out of the flame.
4. Mix almond flour, eggs, and seasonings in a dish and stir.
5. Add meat as well as onions, and then combine using clean hands.
6. Shape into a loaf.

7. Grease your slow cooker with a coconut-oil-based spray.
8. Put the loaf in your slow cooker, making sure there's at least a half-inch space between the meat and the sides of the cooker and that the top of the loaf is flat.
9. Adjacent to the cover of the pan.
10. Heat on high for 180 minutes, so that the meat reaches 150 degrees.
11. If you want the loaf to be substantial and not crumbly, let it sit in the cooker for 15–30 minutes after cooking, with the cooker turned off and the lid removed.
12. Eat!

25. Mixed Veggie Omelet

What we need:
- Six whole eggs
- Four egg whites
- ½ cup almond milk (unsweetened)
- One teaspoon of Italian seasoning
- One mug of fresh kale
- 12 cups chopped onion
- One teaspoon of garlic paste
- ½ cup chopped zucchini
- One mug of red bell pepper
- Use pepper and salt as needed.

Getting ready:
1. In a dish, combine eggs, the white part of the eggs, milk, and seasonings.
2. Include veggies.
3. Grease the slow cooker with a coconut-oil-based spray.
4. Pour the omelet into the cooker.
5. Adjacent to the cover of the pan.
6. Cooking it at a high temperature for 90 minutes. If it isn't set, cook for another 25 minutes.
7. Serve hot!

26. Cheesy Eggs, Bacon, and Cauliflower Hash

What we need:
- ½ cauliflower heads
- Two eggs
- Two slices of bacon
- Half a teaspoon of garlic paste
- 1 cup of water
- ½ cup cheddar cheese
- ½ tablespoon minced chives
- Half a teaspoon of onion powder
- Splash of heavy cream
- Salt as needed.
- Use black pepper for testing.

Getting ready:
1. Break up the cauliflower into florets.
2. Crack eggs into a ramekin and mix with cream, a bit of pepper, and salt as needed.
3. Transfer water into your pressure cooker and insert a steamer basket.

27. Poached Salmon

What we need:
- 2 ounces of water
- 1 tablespoon of a dry white wine
- One bay leaf
- One slender piece of everything:
- -Shallot -Lemon
- 1 troy ounce of each:
- Black peppercorns with salt in the kosher style
- 5–6 sprigs of fresh herbs (include dill, tarragon, and other similar herbs)
- 2 lb. salmon skin-on or 4-6 fillets
- Components of the Garnish
- More salt
- Black pepper that has just been freshly cracked
- Vegetable oil
- Wedges of lemons

Getting ready:

1. The contents of the slow cooker should include wine, water, a bay leaf, shallots, salt, peppercorns, and herbs. Prepare for twenty-five minutes on the highest setting.
2. Salt and pepper should be sprinkled on the apex of the fish. Position it in the cooker so that the skin is facing down.
3. Cover the lid and steam for 45 minutes, checking to see whether it is done. Continue if not done until opaque, potentially up to one hour.
4. If you choose the warm setting, it is appropriate for a few hours' worth of use. Oil and other garnishes should be drizzled over the dish.
5. Enjoy!

28. Cottage Cheese with Nut Medley

What we need:
- ½ cup cottage cheese (full-fat or low-fat, as per preference)
- ¼ cup mixed nuts (e.g., almonds, walnuts, and pecans), roughly chopped
- ½ teaspoon honey (optional, for a touch of sweetness)
- Fresh berries (e.g., strawberries, blueberries, or raspberries) for garnish (optional)

Getting ready:
1. Ensure you have all the ingredients ready for your cottage cheese with nuts. Scoop out the desired amount of cottage cheese and put it in a dish.
2. Roughly chop the variety of nuts of your choice. Almonds, walnuts, and pecans work wonderfully together, providing a mix of textures and flavors. Sprinkle the chopped nuts over the cottage cheese.
3. If you desire a touch of sweetness, add honey over the cottage cheese and nut mixture. Make it as spicy or as mild as you like, or omit it completely for a savory meal.
4. Scatter some fresh berries on top for an additional splash of color, taste, and nutrients. Strawberries, blueberries, and raspberries complement the creaminess of the cottage cheese and the crunch of the nuts.
5. Your Cottage Cheese with Nut Medley is ready to enjoy. Each spoonful combines the creamy richness of cottage cheese with the satisfying crunch of mixed nuts and the subtle sweetness of honey (if used). Fresh berries bring a delicious balance of tartness and juicy sweetness.
6. Feel free to get creative with your cottage cheese and nut medley. Experiment with different nut varieties, adjust the sweetness level, or try different combinations of fresh fruits.

29. Vegetable Korma

What we need:
- Florets from one whole head's worth of cauliflower
- 3/4 tablespoons of full-fat coconut milk from a 10-ounce can
- 2 cups of beans that have been grated
- ½ minced onions were used.
- Two cloves of garlic that have been minced
- As required, pepper and salt may be used.
- Curry powder to the amount of two teaspoons
- Coconut flour to the extent of two teaspoons
- One tsp. garam masala

Getting ready:
1. In your slow cooker, add the various veggies.
2. Combine the ingredients with the coconut milk.
3. Place the mixture in the slow cooker.
4. Sprinkle on top of the coconut flour, then combine everything well.
5. Within close proximity to the lid of the pan.
6. Putting it on steam for a period.
7. Try it out, and add extra seasoning if it needs it.
8. Serve!

30. Zucchini Soup

What we need:
- There should be 3 cups of vegetable stock.
- 2 kg of zucchini that has been chopped
- Two cloves of garlic that have been minced
- 1 and a half tablespoons of minced onion 14 tablespoons of basil leaves
- ½ milliliters of vegetable oil
- As required, pepper and salt may be used.

Getting ready:
1. Take a cooker and warm the vegetable oil over medium to low heat.
2. Stir-fry the garlic and onion together for around five minutes in the heated cooker.
3. The remaining components should then be poured into your heater.
4. Within close proximity to the lid of the pan.
5. Preparing it over a period of two hours at a low temperature.
6. When the allotted time has passed, use a standard blender to purée the soup in stages.

7. Taste them and season them with more pepper and salt, if necessary.

LUNCH

31. Grilled Chicken and Avocado Salad

What we need:

For the salad:
- 3 skinless, boneless breasts of chicken
- 6 cups mixed leaves: spinach, arugula, or your favorite green salad
- 1 ripe, minced avocado
- ½ chopped cucumber
- 1 cup halved tomatoes
- ¼ thinly chopped onion
- Vegetable oil for grilling
- Salt to taste

For the salad dressing:
- 4 tablespoons of vegetable oil
- 1 tablespoon balsamic vinegar
- Pepper to taste
- 1 clove of crushed garlic
- 1 teaspoon Dijon mustard
- Salt to taste

Getting ready:
1. Set the temperature in your oven somewhere between high and medium. Skirmish the breasts with flavor and oil with black pepper and salt.
2. Keep the meat in the preheated oven. Bake for approximately six to seven minutes on each surface. The baking time may differ because it depends on the thickness of your chicken.
3. Remove the meat from the grill and permit it to chill for a few moments to allow the wetness to redistribute. Then, slice the grilled chicken into thin strips.
4. Put a big salad dish; combine the mixed greens, chopped avocado, cucumber, tomatoes, and onion. Take a dish and whip all the elements—mustard, vegetable oil, pepper, salt, vinegar, and garlic—to create the dressing in it.
5. Sprinkle the salad over the mixer and combine gently to coat the ingredients consistently. Organize the chopped chicken, which is grilled on top of the avocado salad.
6. Divide the grilled chicken and avocado salad among serving plates.
7. Enjoy!

32. Cobbler Topped with Chicken Gravy

What we need:

- 2 tablespoons of ghee or unsalted butter (or, if dairy-free, coconut oil);
- 1½ cup of mushrooms, sliced into pieces
- ¼ cup of onion pieces, diced
- 2 celery ribs, thinly sliced and sliced again
- 1 cup of asparagus that has been sliced
- 1 teaspoon of fine-grained salt from the ocean
- Ground dark pepper to the amount of 12 tablespoons
- 4 ounces of cream cheese for the 12 servings
- 3/4 cups of chicken bone juice, scones that were either made locally or purchased from a shop.
- 4 really large egg whites
- 1 cup of almond flour that has been whitened
- 1 teaspoon of the powder used for heating
- ¼ milligram of very fine ocean salt
- 3 tablespoons of frozen margarine (or lard, if dairy-free), cut into small pieces Thyme, fresh and for use in trimming
- Ghee that has been melted and used as a spread or for bathing

Getting ready:

1. Broil at 400 degrees. Medium-heated cast-iron pans soften ghee. Fry the mushrooms and onions until they're darker, and then stir the celery and asparagus for three more minutes.
2. Pepper and salt the sliced chicken breast on both sides. Brown and fry the chicken in a pan. It should be undercooked. Mix the cream cheese in the pan until there are no lumps. Enter the broth rapidly but cautiously. Start making scones for the fixing after storing it.
3. Start by whisking the egg whites in a mixing bowl so that they're firm. Mix the powder, salt, and almond flour in a similar-sized container.
4. After that, mix in the spread. (The scones won't turn out if the spread isn't refrigerated.) Gently spread the flour mixture over the egg whites. Use a big spoon or frozen yogurt scooper to scoop out the dough and shape it into 2-inch scones. Maintain margarine clusters.
5. Mix the bread rolls with the mixture in the pan. Prepare for 12–15 minutes until the bread rolls are black enough. Add thyme and melted butter. Water- or airtight containers can store additional items in the icebox for three days. It should be cooked well in a dish.

33. Deviled Egg with Pickled Jalapenos

What we need:
- Canola mayonnaise (¼ cup)
- Jalapeno pepper rings (2 tablespoons)
- 1 tablespoon Creole mustard
- 1 teaspoon Sriracha (hot bean stew sauce)
- Ground dark pepper (¼ teaspoon)
- 4 hard-cooked enormous eggs, stripped
- 4 Boston lettuce leaves
- 2 tablespoons slashed green onion tops

Getting ready:
1. Consolidate the initial five ingredients into a bowl.
2. Cut the eggs down the middle and evacuate the yolk. Finely slash the egg white; press the yolk through a strainer using the back of a spoon.
3. Tenderly overlay the egg with the mayonnaise blend. Top every lettuce leaf with about 14 cups of mixed greens and 112 teaspoons of green onion tops.

34. Herb Pesto Pork Chops

What we need:
- Bread crumbs (½ cup)
- (3-ounce) pork top-loin chops
- Vegetable oil (1 tablespoon)
- Herb Pesto (8 teaspoons)

Getting ready:
1. Set the oven and prepare an oven sheet by lining it with parchment or foil.
2. Place the loaf crumbs in a trivial dish to spread them out evenly.
3. Coat each pork chop in bread crumbs, turning to ensure a uniform coating on both sides. Remove any extra crumbs by shaking.
4. In a large pan that is heated, bring the vegetable oil to the desired temperature.
5. The breaded pork chops need to be cooked for about three to four minutes on both sides so that they have a color that is similar to a golden brown.
6. Arrange the pork chops in a particular coating on a piece of baking parchment and complete the cooking process in the oven.
7. Cover the top of each pork chop with two teaspoons' worth of the herb pesto and set aside.
8. Set the chops in an oven that has been prepared and roast for about 12 to 15 minutes, so that they are suitable for eating well.

9. The pork chops are done when they are removed from the heated oven and allowed to chill for a few moments before being served.
10. Warm the herb pesto pork chops and serve them with roasted vegetables, mashed potatoes, or a fresh salad, as desired.

35. Beef Stir-up

What we need:
- Lean ground beef (½ pound)
- Shredded cabbage (½ cup)
- Herb Pesto (¼ cup)
- 6 hamburger buns
- Sweet onion (½ cup)

Getting ready:
1. Warm oil in a big cooker on medium heat.
2. Slice a sweet onion and sauté it in the pan until it becomes transparent and caramelized.
3. The onions should be moved to one side of the pan, and the ground beef should be added to the other.
4. To ensure the ground beef is well cooked, brown it in a skillet while breaking it up with a spoon.
5. Shredded cabbage should be added to the pan with the ground meat and onions. Add two to three more minutes of cooking time to get a tiny wilt out of the cabbage.
6. Put the flame on low and mix in the herb pesto. The pesto should be well mixed into the steak and cabbage.
7. Let it steam for a few minutes so the flavors can combine.
8. As the beef mixture cooks, toast the buns in the oven until they are golden brown and crunchy.
9. Turn off the heat after the meat combination has reached the desired doneness for you.
10. To assemble the beef stir-up, spread the bottom halves of the toasted hamburger buns with mayonnaise and then heap a heaping spoonful of the beef and cabbage mixture on top.
11. To finish the sandwiches, put the top halves of the buns on the canopy of the beef mixture.
12. Beef stir-up is ready to be served as a savory and filling supper right away.

36. Adobo Chicken

What we need:
- 1 pound of chicken
- Two tablespoons of adobo sauce
- 1 tablespoon of flour
- 0.75 cups cheddar
- 0.5 cups salsa
- 1 tablespoon of butter
- 0.5 cups of milk

Getting ready:
1. Mix adobo and salsa.
2. Place it in the pressure cooker.
3. Add chicken.
4. Cook on low for a total of eight hours.
5. Tear the chicken into shreds.
6. In a separate cooker, heat the butter.
7. Mix flour.
8. Stir in milk.
9. Stir until there are no lumps.
10. 10: Mix in the cheese while stirring.
11. Continue to stir until a thick paste forms.
12. Place the mixture in the slow cooker.
13. Give the flavors some time to combine.

37. Beef Bread

What we need:
- Lean ground beef (1 pound)
- White vinegar
- Bread crumbs (½ cup)
- One large egg
- Chopped basil (2 tablespoons)
- ½ cup sweet onion
- 1 teaspoon diced thyme
- Garlic paste
- 1 teaspoon minced parsley
- ¼ teaspoon of black pepper

- Brown sugar

Getting ready:
1. After spraying or oiling a loaf cooker with butter, set it in the oven to preheat until the temperature reaches 350 degrees Fahrenheit (175 degrees Celsius).
2. Combine the ground beef, bread crumbs, egg, white vinegar, thyme, parsley, black pepper, and garlic paste in a big mixing dish.
3. Distribute the spices evenly throughout the meat by using either your clean hands or a spoon to properly combine everything.
4. Make a loaf shape with the meat combination and set it into the heated loaf pan.
5. To add a little sweetness during baking, sprinkle a thin coating of brown sugar across the meatloaf.
6. Roast the meatloaf for thirty to thirty-five minutes at the measurement temperature.
7. Slice and serve the meatloaf a few minutes after removing it from the oven.
8. Warm the delicious meatloaf pieces and serve with your preferred dishes and a healthy salad or mashed potatoes.
9. Indulge in the savory taste of this meatloaf made with lean ground beef, fragrant herbs, and a brown sugar topping.

38. Crispy Chicken

What we need:
- Half-cup avocado oil
- ½ cup country dressing—homemade or store-bought
- 3-tablespoon coconut aminos
- 1 tablespoon minced garlic
- Coconut vinegar
- Lemon juice
- 1 teaspoon ground dark pepper
- 4 pieces of skinless, boneless chicken breast
- 2 tablespoons of coconut or avocado oil for parmesan sauce
- ½ cup country dressing—homemade
- ¼ cup ground Parmesan cheddar parmesan beating
- ½ cup pork dust (or whitened almond flour if sensitive) 1/3 cup ground Parmesan cheddar
- Unsalted margarine and dissolved garlic salt
- Melted Provolone cheddar

Getting ready:
1. Marinade the ingredients in a shallow dish. Mix chicken thighs with fleece. Spread and marinate in the refrigerator for an hour.

2. Preheat your microwave. Discard the marinade, slap lightly the meat waterless, and then flavor all sides with pepper, salt, and spices.
3. Place a cooker over high-medium heat; deep-fry the meat for three minutes in coconut oil. Flip and heat until done.
4. Prepare Parmesan sauce: Mix ½ cup farm dressing and ¼ cup Parmesan cheddar in a dish.
5. In another small dish, combine pork dust, 1/3 cup Parmesan cheddar, liquefied margarine, and garlic salt for the Parmesan pounding. Combine well.
6. Spread the chicken in the pan with Parmesan sauce, top with provolone cheddar, and then spray with parmesan besting. Put it on the burner after sautéing for four minutes so that the cheddar melts and the fixing darkens.
7. Store extra products in an airtight icebox compartment for 3 days.

39. Persian Chicken

What we need:
- 5 chicken thighs, boneless
- Ground cumin (½ teaspoon)
- ½ sweet onions
- Oregano (1 tablespoon)
- 1 teaspoon garlic
- Pressed lemon juice (¼ cup)
- Sweet paprika (1 teaspoon)
- Vegetable oil

Getting ready:
1. Ground cumin, chopped sweet onion, dried oregano, minced garlic, lemon juice, oil, salt, sweet paprika, and black pepper should all be combined in a mixing dish. Marinate the chicken by thoroughly combining the ingredients.
2. Boneless chicken thighs should be placed in a dish that can be sealed.
3. Make sure every piece of chicken is doused with marinade. To ensure that the marinade is well distributed, you should massage it into the chicken.
4. Put the chicken in the fridge, covered, for at least two hours to marinate and soak up the spices.
5. Prepare an oven by heating it to high-medium.
6. Take the meat out of the soak and let the extra liquid drain out.
7. Bake the chicken for approximately five to six minutes per side.
8. To maximize wetness and zest retention, stitch the chicken with the soak while it bakes.

9. Once the chicken thighs have finished grilling, remove them to a tray to chill for two minutes before enjoying. Saffron rice, baked veggies, or a crisp salad would all go well with the Special Persian Chicken.
10. Fresh herbs like parsley make for a visually appealing and flavorful garnish. Tender and juicy, the Special Persian Chicken is bursting with flavor and perfume.

40. Special Noodles

What we need:
- A quarter of a pound's worth of dry soba noodles
- Nut Sesame Sauce
- 1/3 cup julienne-cut pickling cucumber
- ¼ cup matchstick-cut carrots
- Two teaspoons of green onions that have been pre-sliced
- 1 teaspoon of sesame seeds (optional), if desired.

Getting ready:
1. Follow the package directions for cooking the soba noodles.
2. Preparing the peanut-sesame sauce can be started while the noodles are cooking.
3. Drain and wash them in lukewarm water while they are running. Put the noodles, carrots, cucumber, and green onions into a medium bowl and mix them all together. Sprinkle on some peanut-sesame sauce, and then carefully toss everything to cover it.
4. It can be served at room temperature or spread out and chilled . If you like, you may improve it by adding sesame seeds.

41. Fried Rice with Cauliflower

What we need:
- 2 cups of medium-sized cauliflower heads chopped into floated
- 2 tablespoons of sesame oil
- 1 finely chopped onion
- 3 cloves of minced garlic
- 1 small carrot, nicely sliced
- ½ cup frozen peas
- 2 large, beaten eggs
- 3 tablespoons of soy sauce
- ½ teaspoon ground ginger
- To taste, black pepper and salt
- Sliced green onions
- Sesame seeds (optional, for garnish)

Getting ready:
1. Wash and thoroughly dry the cauliflower head. Cut it into florets. Using a cooker, fry the cauliflower until it is well mixed with the rice. Our goal is a texture similar to rice, not puree, so be careful not to overcook.
2. Warm the oil in a cooker over high heat. Mix the garlic with the onion. Stir for two to three minutes, waiting for them to become fragrant and translucent.
3. Swirl in the finely chopped carrot with frozen peas. Keep frying for another couple of minutes, or until the veggies begin to get tender. Move the sautéed vegetables to one side of the cooker, creating an empty space.
4. Pour the whisked eggs into the vacant spot. Scramble the eggs with a spatula so that they are cooked through but moist a little. This should take about 2 minutes.
5. Mix the scrambled eggs with the sautéed vegetables. Mix the rice in the cooker. Put the leftover sesame oil over the cauliflower rice.
6. Season the mixture with black pepper soy sauce, salt, and ground ginger. Stir everything together thoroughly.
7. Cook the cauliflower rice for five to seven minutes, moving irregularly, and the rice should become a little affectionate but not mushy.
8. Take the cooker off the flame as soon as the cauliflower rice has reached the consistency that you want to consume. If you want, you may sprinkle some chopped onions and toasted sesame seeds on top.
9. Enjoy!

42. Cauliflower and broccoli soup

What we need:
- 1 head of cauliflower, chopped
- 1 head of broccoli, chopped
- 1 chopped small onion
- 2 cloves of minced garlic
- 4 cups of vegetable or chicken broth
- ½ cup heavy cream
- 2 tablespoons of vegetable oil
- Black pepper and salt to taste
- Fresh chives or parsley, for garnish (optional)

Getting ready:
1. Dice the broccoli and cauliflower into small pieces. The vegetable oil should be heated in a large cooker over high heat.
2. Sauté the vegetables for two to three minutes, so that they release a fragrant aroma and become open and forthcoming. The florets of cauliflower and broccoli should be added

to the saucepan. Stir them in with the sautéed onion and garlic, and keep cooking for two or three minutes more.

3. Transfer the chicken soup to cover the vegetables. If needed, add a bit more broth to ensure the vegetables are submerged.
4. Stir the ingredients all the way up to boiling, and then turn the heat into steam. The cauliflower and broccoli should be cooked for around fifteen to twenty minutes with the lid on the pot before they are soft and can be readily punctured with a fork.
5. Whip everything together in a blender until it reaches a velvety consistency. If you were using a blender, put the soup that has been puréed back into the cooker.
6. Swirl in the heavy cream to add extra creaminess to the soup. Grind some black pepper and add salt to taste.
7. Warm the soup above simmering, whisking it from time to time, while it is at the desired temperature. Be careful not to boil it once the cream is added. Ladle the warm cauliflower and broccoli soup into soup dishes. If you wish, decorate with minced fresh chives for a pop of flavor and color.
8. Serve this comforting and nutritious soup as a starter or a light meal. It's creamy, satisfying, and packed with the goodness of cauliflower and broccoli.

43. Stuffed Vegetables with Mushroom

What we need:
- 3 large bell peppers, any color
- 1 tablespoon of vegetable oil
- finely chopped 1 onion
- 8 ounces chopped mushrooms
- 2 cups fresh, chopped spinach
- 2 cups of quinoa (boiled)
- 1 cup mozzarella cheese
- ½ teaspoon oregano
- pepper and salt, to taste

Getting ready:
1. Slice the bell peppers. Set the prepared peppers aside.
2. Cook vegetable oil on low in a cooker. Mix and twirl the onion for 2–3 minutes until lucent. Add garlic and simmer until fragrant.
3. Add finely minced mushrooms and sauté until they are dried and turn a golden brown color. Incorporate minced spinach and allow it to simmer for 2–3 minutes until it has wilted and season with black pepper, dried oregano, and salt.
4. If you're using quinoa, stir it into the mushroom and spinach mixture. Mix until everything is nicely mixed.

5. Mix in the shredded mozzarella cheese once it melts, while the mixture is held together by the cheese's melted consistency. Carefully load each bell pepper with the combination of mushrooms, spinach, and quinoa (or cauliflower rice) until they are completely full.
6. If you choose, you may add an additional layer of taste to each filled pepper by spreading crumbled Parmesan on top of it. Put the bell peppers that have been packed on a baking tray. The dish should be covered with aluminum foil. It should be baked in an oven that has been warmed for around thirty to twenty-five minutes until all of the veggies are soft.
7. Take off the foil and carry on cooking for five to ten minutes more so that the tops are slightly browned.
8. Serve.

44. Quiche Lorraine

What we need:
- 2 strips of bacon, diced
- 3 huge eggs
- 3/4 cup cashew milk
- 14 cups unflavored egg white protein powder
- 1 teaspoon of prepared powder
- 1 teaspoon of fine ocean salt
- 2 teaspoons diced new chives
- ½ cup sharp cheddar (or dietary yeast if without dairy), isolated

Getting ready:
1. Bring the temperature on the stovetop up to 425 degrees Fahrenheit.
2. Spot the diced bacon in a heated cooker. Set the flame over high heat and boil the bacon the bacon so that it is fresh for around five minutes. Remove half of the bacon and set aside the drippings in the skillet; set aside the remaining bacon.
3. In a blender, combine the eggs, cashew milk, protein powder, heating powder, and salt. Mix for around 1 minute, until frothy, and include the chives and 14 cups of cheddar. Empty the blend into the hot skillet over the bacon.
4. Move the cooker and prepare for 10 minutes. Expel from the broiler and top with more cheddar.
5. Heat for an additional 10 minutes so that the outside layer is gasping and darker. Slice into wedges and decorate with the saved bacon.
6. Store additional items in a hermetically sealed compartment in the fridge for as long as 3 days.
7. Warm on a rimmed heating sheet in a 350°F stove until warmed through.

45. Chicken Gyros

What we need:
- Five onions
- 2 kg of chicken breast in ground form
- 5 cups breadcrumbs
- One and one-fourth teaspoons of thyme
- 25 teaspoons worth of ground nutmeg
- One and a half teaspoons of vegetable oil
- Three whole cloves of garlic
- Two eggs
- One lemon
- Cinnamon equals 25 tablespoons.
- 12 pita breads

Toppings:
- Greek yogurt with tomato, cucumber, and lemon in its simple form

Getting ready:
1. Prepare the garlic and onion by processing them.
2. Combine the aforementioned ingredients together with the eggs, lemon, cinnamon, salt, breadcrumbs, thyme, and nutmeg. Mix well.
3. Roll into a ball.
4. Toss it into the slow cooker.
5. Heat vegetable oil.
6. Cook on low for a total of 8 hours.
7. When everything is done, place it on a pita, and then add the toppings.

46. Chicken Satay

What we need:
- 2 lime juice
- Chicken breast (12 ounces)
- 2 tablespoons brown sugar
- Cumin
- 1 tablespoon minced garlic

Getting ready:
1. Mix the lime juice, brown sugar, cumin, garlic, salt, and pepper together in a bowl. Combine ingredients to make a marinade.
2. To the marinade, add the chicken breast strips, turning to coat each piece well.

3. To bring out the most flavor in the chicken, marinate it for at least 30 minutes, preferably overnight.
4. Prepare a microwave by heating it over high heat.
5. Marinated meat pieces are threaded onto skewers with enough room between them.
6. Prepare the chicken skewers by grilling them for three to four minutes per side, so that they are well cooked. If you want to avoid sticking or shattering them, be careful while turning them.
7. Any residual marinade may be used to baste the chicken as it grills for an added dose of flavor and moisture.
8. After the skewers have finished cooking, take them out of the microwave and set the meat side to rest for a few minutes.
9. When eaten with peanut sauce or any dipping sauce of your choice, the Asian Chicken Satay is a versatile dish that works well both as an appetizer and as a main course.
10. Serve the satay with steamed rice and a side salad for a filling supper.
11. Asian Chicken Satay, marinated in lime juice and flavored with fragrant spices, is delicate and tasty.

47. Pork Chops

What we need:
- Bread crumbs (½ cup)
- (3-ounce) pork top-loin chops
- Vegetable oil (1 tablespoon)
- Herb Pesto (8 teaspoons)

Getting ready:
1. Set the oven and prepare an oven sheet by lining it with parchment or foil.
2. Put the bread crumbs in a dish and spread them out evenly.
3. Coat each pork chop in bread crumbs, turning to ensure a uniform coating on both sides. Remove any extra crumbs by shaking.
4. In a large pan that is heated, bring the vegetable oil to the desired temperature.
5. The breaded pork chops need to be cooked for about three to four minutes on both sides so that they have a color that is similar to a golden brown.
6. Arrange the pork chops in a layer on a sheet of baking parchment and complete the cooking process in the oven.
7. Cover the top of each pork chop with two teaspoons' worth of the herb pesto and set aside.
8. Place the chops in an oven that has been prepared and steam for approximately 12 to 15 minutes, so that the meats are well cooked.

9. The pork chops are done when they are removed from the microwave and allowed to chill for a few minutes before being served.
10. Warm the herb pesto pork chops and serve them with roasted vegetables, mashed potatoes, or a fresh salad, as desired.

48. Chicken loaf

What we need:
- Chicken (2 pounds)
- White vinegar
- Bread crumbs (½ cup)
- One large egg
- Chopped basil (2 tablespoons)
- Sweet onion (½ cup)
- thyme (1 teaspoon)
- Garlic paste
- Minced parsley (2 teaspoon)
- ¼ teaspoon of black pepper
- Brown sugar

Getting ready:
1. After spraying or oiling a loaf cooker with a spray of butter, preheat the oven.
2. Combine the ground chicken, bread crumbs, egg, white vinegar, thyme, parsley, garlic paste, and black pepper in a basin.
3. Spoon to properly combine everything.
4. Make a loaf shape with the meat combination and put it into the heated loaf pan.
5. To add a little sweetness during baking, sprinkle a thin coating of brown sugar over the top of the meatloaf.
6. Bake the meatloaf for 50 to 60 minutes so that it gets a golden brown color.
7. Slice and serve the meatloaf a few minutes after removing it from the oven.
8. Warm the delicious meatloaf pieces and serve with your preferred dishes and a healthy salad or mashed potatoes.
9. Indulge in the savory taste of this meatloaf made with lean ground beef, fragrant herbs, and a brown sugar topping.

49. Granola and Grilled Peaches

What we need:
- Peaches, cut in half and pitted: 4
- Spray the oven.
- Eight servings of a salad mix.
- Raspberry Vinaigrette Dressing, Light, 1⁄3 Cups
- Raspberries, fresh, enough for 1 cup
- ½ pound of blueberries
- ½ cup of roasted, sliced almonds
- Granola with low-fat content, enough for four cups
- Crumbled goat cheese, 1 cup (4 ounces)

Getting ready:
1. The grill should be heated to around medium.
2. Spray cooking spray on the cut peach halves. Arrange peaches, cut sides up, on a frying rack that has been sprayed with cooking oil.
3. Peach halves need 3 minutes on the grill per side to get grill marks. Make four equal wedges out of each peach half.
4. Toss the salad greens with vinaigrette and serve them in a basin. Gently swirl in the berries, granola, and almonds.
5. Distribute the salad ingredients so that each of the four salad plates has 2.5 cups.
6. Put 8 peach wedges on each plate and sprinkle each with 2 tablespoons of cheese.

50. Zesty Mediterranean Chicken Thighs

What we need:
- 5 chicken thighs, boneless
- Ground cumin (½ teaspoon)
- ½ sweet onions
- Oregano (1 tablespoon)
- 1 teaspoon garlic
- Pressed lemon juice (¼ cup)
- Sweet paprika (1 teaspoon)
- Vegetable oil

Getting ready:
1. Combine ground cumin, chopped sweet onion, dried oregano, minced garlic, lemon juice, sweet paprika, salt, vegetable oil, and pepper in a mixing dish. Marinate the chicken by thoroughly combining the ingredients.
2. Boneless chicken thighs should be placed in a dish that can be sealed.

3. Make sure every piece of chicken is doused with marinade. To ensure that the marinade is well distributed, you should massage it into the chicken.
4. Let the chicken sit in the marinade, covered, for at least two hours so the flavors may soak in.
5. Prepare a microwave pan by heating it to high.
6. Take the chicken out of the marinade and let the extra liquid drain out.
7. To ensure well cooked chicken, heat for around 5 to 6 minutes on each side.
8. To maximize flavor and moisture retention, baste the chicken with the marinade while it grills.
9. Once the chicken thighs have finished grilling, remove them to a tray to chill them for a few minutes before enjoying.

51. Beef Bourguignon

What we need:
- 2 kg of grass-fed beef stew meat
- One bottle of dry red wine measuring 750 milliliters
- Four cups' worth of chopped mushrooms
- Eight individual pieces of bacon
- A single chopped onion.
- Butter from grass-fed cows, whipped into three tablespoons
- Three garlic cloves that have been minced
- A pair of bay leaves
- A quarter of a teaspoon's worth of dried thyme
- One spoonful of tomato paste (no sugar added)
- Parsley, dry, one-half of a teaspoonful
- The appropriate amount of pepper and salt

Getting ready:
1. In the event that the meat has not yet been chopped, chunk it up.
2. Sprinkle generously with black pepper and salt.
3. In a separate cooker, melt 2 tablespoons of butter.
4. Following that, mix the steak and fry it for three minutes.
5. After removing the meat, set it in a cooker.
6. Include bacon, and fry it until it's browned and crispy.
7. Remove the bacon and cut it into thin slices.
8. A small amount of red wine should be added to the skillet.
9. Put the bacon in the heater, and then pour the ingredients from the skillet as well as the remainder of the wine into it.

10. Combine all of the ingredients when you've added them.
11. Prepare it by simmering it at a low temperature for eight to ten hours, until the meat is easy to chew.

52. Classic Pot Roast

What we need:
- 2-3 lbs. beef chuck roast
- 4 cloves garlic, minced
- Salt to taste
- 2 tablespoons of vegetable oil
- 1 cup chopped onion
- 4 cups of beef broth
- pepper to taste
- 3 large carrots, cut into chunks
- 4-5 potatoes, cut into chunks
- 3 celery stalks, chopped
- 2-3 sprigs of fresh thyme
- 2 bay leaves

Getting ready:
1. Season the beef chuck roast generously with salt and pepper on all sides.
2. The vegetable oil should be heated over medium-high heat in a big Dutch oven or heavy-bottomed saucepan.
3. Sear the roast for four to five minutes each side, or until browned. The roast should be removed from the heat and placed aside.
4. Chopped garlic and onion should be added to the same saucepan. For around 5 minutes, sauté until they become tender and fragrant.
5. Toss in the beef broth and red wine, if using, and scrape the pan bottom for any browned bits. Simmer it for a few minutes to slightly reduce the liquid.
6. Spoon the browned roast back into the saucepan. Arrange the celery, potatoes, and carrots around the roast.
7. Tuck the fresh thyme, rosemary, and bay leaves into the broth around the meat and vegetables.
8. Cover the pot with a lid and place it in a preheated oven at 325°F (165°C). To achieve delicate, easily-falling-apart beef, cook for three to four hours.
9. After taking the pot out of the oven, carefully remove the roast. Let it rest for a few minutes before slicing or shredding.
10. Discard the bay leaves and herb sprigs.
11. Serve the pot roast with the cooked vegetables and some of the rich broth from the pot.

53. Paneer Curry with Stuffed Potatoes

What we need:
- 2 potatoes pre-cut for the microwave
- Spray the oven.
- Vegetable oil, 1 teaspoon
- Half a cup of chopped onion
- 1.25 ounces of diced tomato
- 1 tsp. of curry powder, red
- 1 ml of fresh ginger paste, ground
- A pinch of salt
- 1 cup of chopped spinach leaves from a bag
- Diced paneer, 1 cup (4 ounces)
- Garam Masala, Quarter Teaspoonful

Optional: 1 tablespoon finely chopped fresh cilantro.

Getting ready:
1. Prepare potatoes in the microwave in accordance with package instructions for cooking two potatoes simultaneously.
2. Prepare a big, nonstick pan over medium heat while the potatoes simmer. Spray cooking spray on the pan.
3. Toss some oil into the pan and give it a good stir to coat everything. In the heated oil, mix the onions and stir them for two minutes.
4. After two minutes of cooking, during which time you should stir the mixture often; add the tomato, red curry powder, ginger, and salt. Remove it from the heat immediately. After stirring everything in, wait for the spinach to wilt before serving.
5. Add cheese and garam masala and mix well.
6. To open potatoes, remove their wrappings and then slice them lengthwise. Place approximately a quarter cup of the tomato puree in the center of all the potatoes. Cilantro may be used as a garnish.

54. Different Chicken Curry

What we need:
- 6 chicken thighs, boneless
- Vegetable oil
- Ginger paste (2 teaspoon)
- Coconut milk (¼ cup)
- Garlic (2 teaspoons)
- 1 large Onion minced

- Garam masala (2 tablespoon)
- Water

Getting ready:
1. Fill a large pot with oil and heat it over high heat
2. Fry the chopped cilantro for a minute to bring out its flavor.
3. Salt and pepper the chicken thighs before adding them to the cooker. Stir until brown on all sides, which will take about 5 to 7 minutes.
4. Before removing the chicken from the pan,
5. Put the garlic that has been minced, the onion that has been finely diced, and the ginger that has been grated into the same skillet. It takes around 4 minutes of sautéing for the onion to become transparent and aromatic.
6. Put the water back into the pan, and put the chicken thighs back in. Stir the ingredients together and bring the mixture to a boil.
7. Warp the chicken and steam it slowly on low heat for 20 to 25 minutes, until it is fully cooked and soft.
8. Take off the cover and mix in the curry paste and the milk. Adding more pepper and salt may be necessary.
9. The curry's flavors will improve with an additional 5 minutes of simmering.
10. Eat the Indian chicken curry with some steamed rice and some naan bread. If you want, you can sprinkle some more chopped cilantro on top.
11. Chicken curry from India is a delicious and fragrant main course option.

55. Rice with lentil curry

What we need:
- 1 (8.5-ounce) bundle of microwaveable precooked basmati rice
- 1 (17.63-ounce) bundle of dried petite green lentils
- Half a cup of brilliant raisins
- Red onion, half cup
- Pine nuts, toasted (¼ cup)
- 2 tablespoons broiled garlic rice vinegar
- Curry powder (1 tablespoon)
- Salt (1/8 teaspoon)
- 2 tablespoons of vegetable oil

Getting ready:
1. Place the rice in a sizable bowl and microwave according to the package directions. Include lentils and the next 3 ingredients; hurl tenderly.
2. Join vinegar, salt, and curry powder in a little bowl. Slowly include the oil and additions with a whisk.

3. Pour dressing over the rice blend; hurl delicately. Serve promptly, or spread and refrigerate for 2 hours.

56. Baked Egg

What we need:
- Chopped red peppers (½ cup)
- Parsley
- Zucchini (¼ cup)
- Salt
- Coconut oil (½ tbsp)
- Dried basil
- Green onions, sliced (¼ cup)
- Ground black pepper
- Coconut milk (¼ cup)
- Two eggs
- Almond flour (1/8 cup)

Getting ready:
1. Take a cooker, melt the coconut oil, and heat it.
2. Toss in the chili flakes, zucchini gratings, and green onion slices.
3. To soften the veggies, sauté them for a few minutes.
4. Add some salt, dried basil, and black pepper to the veggies. Combining tastes requires a good stir.
5. Separately, put the coconut milk and eggs in a dish and beat until smooth.
6. Whisk constantly as you add the almond flour to the egg mixture to ensure it is well combined.
7. Place the veggies in an equal layer in a baking dish that has been oiled.
8. Cover the veggies with the egg mixture by pouring it over the top.
9. When the oven is ready, place the baking dish inside and bake for twenty-five to thirty minutes, so that the egg bake is firm and the outer layer is browned.
10. After the dish has finished baking, remove it from the oven and set it aside to cool.
11. Fresh parsley is a great garnish since it adds both color and flavor.
12. Warm the egg bake, cut it into slices, and serve.

57. Tuna and avocado salad

What we need:
- 2 cans of canned tuna
- 2 ripe avocados, diced
- ½ cup diced onion
- ¼ cup chopped fresh parsley
- 2 tablespoons mayonnaise (or Greek yogurt for a lighter option)
- 1 tablespoon of lemon juice
- Salt-black pepper

Getting ready:
1. Transfer the tuna to a large mixing basin. Dice the avocado flesh and cut the ripe avocados. Tuna and diced avocado should be added to the meal.
2. Combine the tuna, avocado, and red onion in a bowl and add the freshly cut cilantro.
1. Fill a small bowl with the Greek yogurt, lemon juice, and a dash of black pepper and salt. Combine the ingredients with a whisk. If you want more heat, feel free to add red pepper flakes.
2. Transfer the avocado, onion, parsley, and tuna to a platter. Cover them with the sauce. Gently stir everything until the sauce thoroughly coats each component.
3. If you prefer your salad cold, cover it and set it aside for 30 minutes. This will give the tastes time to blend. Alternatively, you can serve it immediately if you're in a hurry.
4. Transfer the tuna and avocado salad to serving plates or bowls. This salad is a quick and delicious option for a light and protein-packed meal. It's perfect as a sandwich filling, a wrap, or served on a bed of lettuce as an option.
5. Garnish your tuna and avocado salad with a sprinkle of fresh cilantro or a few extra avocado slices for presentation.

58. Grilled Shrimp and Vegetable Skewers

What we need:

For the Marinade:
- ¼ cup vegetable oil
- 2 tablespoons of lime sap
- crushed garlic- 2 cloves
- dried oregano 1 teaspoon
- black pepper and Salt

For the Skewers:
- 1 pound of large shrimp, peeled and deveined
- 1 cup of mixed-color bell peppers

- 1 zucchini, cut into cubes
- Cherry tomatoes (optional)

Getting ready:
1. To make the marinade, mix the lemon juice, vegetable oil, chopped garlic, salt, dried oregano, and black pepper in a small bowl with a whisk. Set aside.
2. While the wooden skewers are soaking, thread on the bell pepper chunks, red onion chunks, zucchini rounds, and cherry tomatoes (if using). Alternate the ingredients for a colorful and flavorful skewer.
3. Place the assembled skewers in a tray. Sprinkle the marinade across them, ensuring they are evenly coated. To let the flavors combine, cover and chill for 20-30 minutes.
4. Warm up the grill over medium-high heat. To keep food from sticking, make sure the grill edges are clean and well-oiled.
5. Grill the shrimp and veggie sticks that have been marinating. For two to three minutes on each side, grill the shrimp until they are cooked but still soft.
6. After grilling, transfer the skewers to a serving platter. These grilled shrimp and vegetable skewers are a delightful and healthy meal option.
7. Warm them up and serve with a bit of dipping sauce or a crisp green salad. Garnish with a drizzle of extra marinade or a sprinkle of fresh herbs like parsley or cilantro for a burst of color and flavor.

59. Lamb and pork seasoning

What we need:
- Dried oregano
- Ground allspice (1 teaspoon)
- Thyme, dried
- Garlic paste (1½ teaspoons)
- Celery seed (¼ cup)
- 2 tablespoons of onion paste
- Grated black pepper
- Crushed bay leaf (1 teaspoon)

Getting ready:
1. Put the oregano, thyme, onion powder, celery seed, pepper, garlic paste, allspice, and bay leaf into your blender, and then process it several times to combine the ingredients.
2. Transfer the mixture to a container that is both shallow and has a lid.
3. Put them in a spot where they will be dry and cool.

60. Simple Chicken Gravy

What we need:
- 2 tablespoons of ghee or unsalted butter (or, if dairy-free, coconut oil);
- 1½ cup of mushrooms, sliced into pieces
- ¼ cup of onion pieces, diced
- 2 celery ribs, thinly sliced and sliced again
- 1 cup of asparagus that has been sliced
- 1 teaspoon of fine-grained salt from the ocean
- Ground dark pepper to the amount of 12 tablespoons
- 4 ounces of cream cheese for the 12 servings
- 3/4 cups of chicken bone juice, scones that were either made locally or purchased from a shop.
- 4 really large egg whites
- 1 cup of almond flour that has been whitened
- 1 teaspoon of the powder used for heating
- ¼ milligram of very fine ocean salt
- 3 tablespoons of frozen margarine (or lard, if dairy-free), cut into small pieces Thyme, fresh and for use in trimming
- Ghee that has been melted and used as a spread or for bathing

Getting ready:
1. Set the oven to 400 degrees. Ghee softens in cast-iron pans heated to about medium. Fry the mushrooms and onions until they get darker, and then stir the celery and asparagus for three more minutes.
2. Pepper and salt both sides of the sliced chicken breast. In a pan, brown and fry the chicken. It should not be done. In the pan, mix the cream cheese until there are no lumps. Enter the soup quickly, but be careful. After putting it away, you can start making scones with it.
3. To begin, whip the egg whites until they reach a stiff peak. In a jar of about the same size, mix the powder, salt, and almond flour.
4. Then, add the spread and stir. (If the spread isn't cold, the scones won't turn out.) Spread the flour mixture slowly over the egg whites. You can scoop out the dough and make it into 2-inch scones with a big spoon or a frozen yogurt scooper. Keep margarine in clumps.
5. Mix the bread rolls into the pan's mixture. Prepare the bread rolls for 12–15 minutes, so that they are dark enough. Add the thyme and butter that have been melted. Extra things can be kept in the icebox for three days in containers that don't leak water or air. It needs to be cooked thoroughly in the dish.

61. Crab Cakes with Lime Salsa

What we need:
For salsa:
- Red bell pepper (½ cup)
- ½ English cucumbers
- Black pepper
- One lime, chopped
- Cilantro, chopped (1 teaspoon)
- **For crab cakes:**
- Parsley (one tablespoon)
- One small egg
- Queen crab meat (8 ounces)
- Vegetable oil
- Hot sauce
- Bread crumbs (¼ cup)
- One scallion, minced
- Red chili flakes (¼ cup)

Getting ready:
1. Take a bowl, mix the red chili flakes, lime, cucumber, and cilantro, and combine everything together well.
2. Pepper them and set them aside after seasoning them with pepper.
3. To make crab cakes, follow these steps:
4. Take a dish and mix the bread crumbs, scallion, egg, crab, spicy sauce, red pepper, and parsley. Mix the ingredients well.
5. If necessary, add in some more bread crumbs.
6. Form the crumbs into four separate patties and place them in a layer on a platter.
7. Frozen for approximately one hour, place the cakes in the fridge.
8. Take a cooker located over low heat and dot the pan with vegetable oil.
9. Put the crab cakes in the oven and heat them for about 5 minutes per side.
10. Accompany them with a bowl of salsa.

DINNER

62. Blueberry Custard Cake in Lemon Flavor

What we need:
- 6 eggs
- Two tablespoons' worth of grated lemon rind
- One milliliter and one teaspoon of stevia liquid
- A half teaspoon and a half of salt
- 0.5 cups blueberries
- Half a cup and a half of coconut flour
- 1 teaspoon of lemon juice
- 0.5 cups stevia
- Two and a half cups of low-fat cream

Getting ready:
1. After removing the yolks from the eggs, start by preparing the egg whites by beating them with a whisk until they form froth.
2. Start by whisking together the egg yolks, then moving on to the other ingredients (except for the blueberries).
3. Lightly and delicately fold the egg whites into the mixture.
4. Add the butter to the slow cooker and reduce the heat to low.
5. Combine the blueberries with the other ingredients.
6. Prepare the dish by cooking it on low heat for three hours.
7. Wait for the temperature to begin to decline.

63. Rice Pudding

What we need:
- 3 eggs
- 1 teaspoon of pure vanilla essence
- 13.5 ounces of creamy coconut
- Grated nutmeg, 0.5 teaspoons
- 0.25 cups of sweetener
- 7-ounce Miracle Rice

Getting ready:
1. Set your oven. Set aside a medium baking dish greased.
2. Beat eggs and mix vanilla essence. This aromatic ingredient makes rice pudding enticing.

3. Pour the thick coconut cream into the bowl and mix with the eggs and vanilla essence. Mix the ingredients carefully.
4. Nutmeg adds a warm, earthy taste to rice pudding. To distribute spices, whisk gently.
5. Add the ideal sweetness. Add your chosen sweetener to the mixture. Choose your preferred sweetener—sugar, honey, or natural.
6. Rinse Miracle Rice with cool water. This amazing rice alternative gives rice pudding a distinctive texture and is almost calorie-free. Before mixing, drain Miracle Rice.
7. Fold Miracle Rice into the coconut-infused sweetness. Coat every grain with the tasty mixture. Spread the rice pudding combination calmly over the oiled bowl.
8. Put the dish in the preheated oven. Bake the rice pudding for 40–45 minutes so it is it is light brown. After removing the rice pudding from the oven, allow it to cool. Your kitchen will smell delicious, teasing you for the pleasure.
9. Nutmeg on top of chilled rice pudding adds refinement. This improves appearance and taste. Serve the coconut pleasure rice pudding hot or cold. It is creamy, cozy, and delightful in each mouthful.
10. Savor every taste of this creative dessert with family and friends. Expect praise and recipe requests!

64. Rice with Beef Gravy

What we need:
- Extra-lean ground beef (½ pound)
- Beef broth, prepared (1 cup)
- Black pepper
- One sweet onion, chopped
- Thyme, chopped (1 teaspoon)
- Minced garlic
- White rice, uncooked (½ cup)
- ½ cup green beans
- One celery stalk, chopped
- Water

Getting ready:
1. Place the cooker on the flame and set the temperature to medium. Once the cooker is hot, add the meat that has been chopped.
2. Brown the meat by cooking it for a certain length of time until it reaches the desired color.
3. Bring the quantity of extra fat down to a manageable level.
4. After a period of time has elapsed, the next step is to add the garlic and the onion to the cooker.

5. They need a cooking time of around three minutes.
6. After that, put in the rice, the celery, the water, and the beef broth.
7. After bringing the water to a boil, reduce the temperature of the stove.
8. Keep the mixture at a low simmer for around half an hour.
9. After that, toss in the thyme and the green beans, and keep on boiling for three minutes more.
10. Take them out of the area that is burning.
11. Pepper is an excellent seasoning for them to utilize.

65. Shrimp Thermion

What we need:
- A large shrimp, peeled and deveined
- butter 2 tablespoons
- chopped 1 shallot
- 1 clove of garlic, minced
- ½ cup heavy cream
- 1/4 cup grated cheese
- 1 teaspoon paprika
- Salt and pepper to taste
- 2 tablespoons parsley, chopped
- 1 tablespoon of lemon juice
- Cooked rice or pasta for serving (optional)

Getting ready:
1. Melt butter in a large pan over medium heat.
2. Toss in the shrimp and cook for two to three minutes on each side, or until opaque/pink. Take the shrimp out of the pan and set them aside.
3. To the same skillet, add chopped shallot and garlic. Cook 2 minutes until tender and aromatic.
4. Pour in the white wine and boil for 3–4 minutes to decrease by half.
5. Pour in heavy cream, Parmesan, Dijon mustard, and paprika. Stir well and boil for 5 minutes to thicken the sauce.
6. Return cooked shrimp to the pan and stir in sauce to coat.
7. Add salt, pepper, and lemon juice to taste.
8. Add fresh parsley and mix.

66. Roasted Beef Stew

What we need:
- Flour (¼ cup)
- Garlic (2 teaspoons)
- Thyme (1 teaspoon)
- Vegetable oil
- One carrot
- ½ sweet onion, chopped
- Water
- Beef stock, prepared (1 cup)
- 2 celery stalks
- Beef chuck roast, boneless (½ pound)
- 1 teaspoon cornstarch
- Grated black pepper
- 2 tablespoons chopped parsley

Getting ready:
1. Warm the oven up to 350 degrees Fahrenheit.
2. Mix the black pepper and flour in a large freezer bag made of synthetic material, and mix them well.
3. Put the meat chunks in the bag, and then give them a good swirl to coat them.
4. Melt the vegetable oil in the cast-iron casserole dish that can go in the oven. Cook each piece of beef for about five minutes, so that it reaches a light brown color.
5. Take out the steak and place it in a separate bowl or on a dish. Put the onion and garlic in the saucepan, and allow them to simmer for about three minutes.
6. Put them in the saucepan with the beef stock, and then deglaze the pot while washing the ground to remove any residues of the beef stock. On a dish, put some water, some carrots, some celery, some meat drippings, and some thyme.
7. Place the lid on the pot in such a way that it is snug, and then put it in the oven. Set the stew in the microwave and roast for approximately one hour, stirring it periodically.
8. To thicken the sauce, add some cornstarch and whisk it into the simmering stew along with two teaspoons of water. Sprinkle some ground black pepper over them. Garnish them with a little chopped parsley.

67. Soup with Chicken and Noodles

What we need:
- Broth made from chicken (1 and ½ cups).
- Chicken that has been salted and cooked (1 cup)
- Black pepper with carrot (one-fourth of a cup)
- Chicken seasoning (one-fourth of a teaspoon)
- Egg noodles that have not been cooked, 2 ounces

Getting ready:
1. Put the water and broth in the cooker and turn it on steam. They need to have some black pepper, kosher salt, and poultry spice added to them.
2. Prepare the chicken by first stripping it, then chopping the carrot. They should be added to the broth and the noodles.
3. They need to be cooked for around 25 minutes.
4. When it is done, allow it to chill for a few moments and enjoy.

68. Beef in a Stir-Fry

What we need:
- Beef ground lean (one-half pound)
- Shredded cabbage equals one half cup.
- Herb Pesto (one-fourth of a cup)
- 6 buns for hamburgers
- 1 half a cup of diced sweet onion

Getting ready:
1. Cook the steak and onion for around six minutes after adding them to the pan.
2. Cook the cabbage for a further three minutes after placing it in the oven.
3. After adding the pesto, give everything a good toss and cook it for about a minute.
4. They should be divided into six servings, each of which should be served with a hamburger bread half.

69. Walleye Simmered in Basil Cream

What we need:
- 1/4 cup overwhelming cream (or full-fat coconut milk if sans dairy)
- 1/4 cup new basil leaves, in addition to extras for enhancement
- 2 tablespoons ghee or unsalted spread (or coconut oil if sans dairy), partitioned
- ½ cup cleaved onions
- 1 clove of garlic, crushed to glue

- 1 pound of walleye fillets, cleaned and cutted
- 1 teaspoon of salt
- ¼ cup fish or chicken bone soup, handcrafted or locally acquired cherry tomatoes, cut down the middle, for enhancement

Getting ready:
1. Put the cream and basil in a blender and blend until the basil leaves are no longer combined with the cream.
2. Put a cooker on flame to warm it up. After melting the ghee in the hot pan, add the onions and garlic and cook for two minutes, once the onions are clear.
3. The fish pieces should be seasoned with pepper and salt. Mix the stock and cream of basil in the pan with the fish. Stir in order to mix. The fish should be cooked for seven minutes with the lid off so that the meat is dark all the way through and easy to break apart.

70. Cheesy Tuna Casserole

What we need:
- Tuna fish 1 pound
- chopped onion 1 tablespoon
- 1 tablespoon ghee
- 1 clove of garlic minced
- 2 cups cauliflower florets cubed
- 1 cup slashed dill pickles
- 1/3 cup cream cheddar mellowed
- 2 tablespoons mayonnaise, natively constructed or locally acquired
- ½ teaspoons of fine ocean salt
- ¼ teaspoon ground dark pepper
- 1 cup destroyed sharp cheddar (precludes dairy-free) Sliced green onions, for embellishment Chopped crisp parsley, for topping
- Cherry tomatoes, divided or quartered, contingent upon the size, for embellishment

Getting ready:
1. Add the onion in the heated cooker and fry for 3 minutes. Stir in the garlic and simmer for a further minute or so.
2. Put the vegetables in a medium-sized bowl that can be used for mixing. Mix the fish, broccoli, pickles, cream cheese, mayonnaise, pepper, and salt into the combination of vegetables. Next, combine the cream cheese, mayonnaise, pepper, and salt.
3. Put the fish combination on the plate that has been lubricated with goulash. If you're using cheddar, crumble some of it over the top. Prepare the dish for twenty minutes, so that the cauliflower is warm and the top of the dish has a little caramelization.

4. Remove it from the heat and give it a five-minute rest. Green onions, parsley, and cherry tomatoes should be used as garnishes before serving.
5. This meal is at its finest when served fresh, but any leftovers may be stored in a container that is hermetically sealed and placed in the refrigerator for up to three days.
6. It should be warmed for three minutes in a dish that has been prepared and placed in a broiler that has been preheated to 350 degrees Fahrenheit.

71. Ginger Beef Salad

What we need:
- Grated ginger (1 tablespoon)
- Vegetable oil
- Flank steak (½ pound)
- Pressed lime juice (2 tablespoons)
- Minced garlic
- **For vinaigrette:**
- Rice vinegar (¼ cup)
- Chopped thyme (1 teaspoon)
- 1 lime juice
- Vegetable oil (¼ cup)
- Zest of 1 lime
- Honey

For salad:
- Green leaf lettuce (4 cups)
- ½, red onion
- Sliced radishes (½ cup)

Getting ready:
1. Put the garlic, ginger, and lime sap in a dish, then mix the vegetable oil and stir it until it's combined. Marinate the steak, and then flip it over so that the marinade can cover all sides of the meat.
2. Put a lid on the bowl, and then put it inside the fridge to marinate the meat. After one hour, take the steak from the refrigerator and put it on the grill after ensuring that it has been preheated.
3. Grill the meat for approximately five minutes per side. The steaks should be left to rest for about ten minutes after being placed on the cutting board.
4. Cut the steak into very thin slices.
5. Place the lime sap, vegetable oil, vinegar, honey, lime zest, and thyme Take a bowl; and give everything a good mix before setting it aside.

6. Place one onion, one radish, and one head of lettuce on each of the six plates, and divide them up evenly.
7. Vinaigrette should be drizzled over the salad. Slice some of the steak and use it as a garnish on top.

72. French Onion Soup

What we need:
- Onions, sliced thin
- Chopped thyme (1 tablespoon)
- Chicken stock (2 cups)
- Ground black pepper
- 2 cups of water
- Unsalted butter

Getting ready:
1. Butter should be melted in a big pan at a temperature that is about equivalent to room temperature. After a certain amount of time has passed, add the onions to the pot, and then proceed to cook them while often flipping them over.
2. Cook for thirty minutes, so that the onions have achieved a stage in which they have been caramelized.
3. Subsequently, bring the broth to a boil, followed by the chicken broth and water. Keep making the stew until it reaches the consistency you want.
4. The soup should be allowed to simmer for around 15 minutes after the heat is reduced to a low setting. After that, add the thyme and give everything a thorough stir before serving.
5. Pepper is the perfect ingredient to use to season them. They should be served as quickly as you can.

73. Traditional Chicken-Vegetable Soup

What we need:
- Unsalted butter
- Ground black pepper
- ½ diced sweet onion
- Chicken stock, cup
- Thyme, chopped (one teaspoon)
- Two celery stalks, chopped
- Parsley (two tablespoons)
- One carrot, diced

- Minced garlic (2 teaspoons)
- 2 cups boiled chicken breast, chopped
- Water

Getting ready:
1. Dissolve the butter in the pan by putting it on low heat. Fry the garlic and onion for three minutes in a pan.
2. Mix carrot, celery, and chicken stock after some time have passed. Start the soup by boiling it.
3. Reduce heat to low and simmer for about 30 minutes. After that, add the thyme, and keep the soup on low heat for another two minutes.
4. For seasoning, pepper is great. Use some fresh parsley as a garnish.

74. Grilled Chicken and Vegetable Stir-Fry

What we need:

For the Marinade:
- 3 skinless, boneless breasts of chicken, sliced and seasoned with pepper and salt
- 2 teaspoons of vegetable oil
- Soy sauce 2 tablespoons
- finely minced 1 garlic clove
- Florets of broccoli to the quantity of 2 cups
- 1 bell pepper, sliced
- 1 carrot, thinly sliced
- ½ thinly chopped onion
- 3 tablespoons of vegetable oil
- 1 cubed bell pepper
- 1 small cubed zucchini
- 1 small yellow squash, sliced

Getting ready:
1. Take a bowl and mix the soy sauce, vegetable oil, garlic, black pepper, grated ginger, and salt by whisking all of the ingredients together.
2. After placing the chicken strips in a container or bag with a zip-top lid, marinate them by pouring the marinade over them.
3. To fully develop the flavors, place the dish or bag in the refrigerator for at least twenty minutes with the lid on or the bag sealed.
4. Prepare the grill for heat between medium and high, or warm a large cooker high flame. If you are using a cooker, add the vegetable oil to the cooker before beginning cook.

5. If you are going to cook the chicken strips on a grill, thread them onto skewers first, then marinade them, and then grill them for approximately three to four minutes on each side, so that they are completely cooked through and have grill marks.
6. If you are using a skillet, add the chicken strips and cook them for approximately three to four minutes on each side, so that they are fully cooked through and have a light browning. Before setting aside, remove the pan from the heat.
7. The vegetable oil should be used to coat the florets of broccoli, slices of bell pepper, zucchini, yellow squash, carrots, and red onion that have been placed in a big bowl. Add some salt and grated black pepper.

75. Grilled Portobello Mushrooms with Spinach and Feta

What we need:
- 4 substantial caps of mushrooms
- 2 cups of spinach leaves that are fresh
- ½ cup of feta cheese in crushed form
- 2 garlic cloves, chopped or minced
- 2 teaspoons of vegetable oil
- A dash of black pepper and salt, to taste

Getting ready:
1. Prepare the grill for cooking over medium-high heat. Garlic that has been minced should be combined with vegetable oil in a cooker.
2. To prepare the Portobello mushroom caps, brush them with vegetable oil that has been infused with garlic, then flavor them with black pepper and salt.
3. Cook the mushrooms on the grill for about four to five minutes pepper side, so that they are soft. Each mushroom cap should have some fresh spinach leaves and a sprinkling of crumble cheese added to it during the last minute of the grilling process.
4. Continue to grill for one minute, turning once, until the spinach is floppy and the cheese is melted.
5. A wholesome and pleasant meal may be made by combining grilled Portobello mushrooms with spinach and feta cheese.

76. Zucchini Noodles with Pesto and Cherry Tomatoes

What we need:
- 2 zucchinis of a manageable size
- 1 cup of cherry tomatoes, cut in half
- A half cup's worth of fresh basil leaves
- ¼ chopped cheddar cheese
- 2 individual garlic cloves

- A quarter cup of pine nuts
- ¼ cup of vegetable oil
- Black pepper and salt, to taste

Getting ready:
1. Make noodles out of the zucchinis by passing them through a spiralizer, and then put them aside.
2. Put the fresh basil, chopped cheddar cheese, garlic, pine nuts, and oil in a grinder and blend so that everything is mixed. Blend until you get a pesto sauce that is completely smooth. Black pepper and salt may be added to taste as a seasoning.
3. Heat a small quantity of vegetable oil in a big cooker over medium heat. Stir the zoodles made from zucchini and the cherry tomatoes. Cook the noodles for around two to three minutes so that they reach the desired degree of tenderness.
4. Combine the zoodles made from zucchini and cherry tomatoes with the pesto sauce that has been prepared.
5. Serve!

77. Baked Salmon with Lemon-Dill Sauce

What we need:
- 4 pieces of salmon fillet
- 2 teaspoons of vegetable oil
- chopped 3 garlic cloves
- lemon sap, freshly squeezed 1 tablespoon
- ½ teaspoon of lemon zest
- A dash of black pepper and salt, to taste

Getting ready:
1. Prepare a temperature in your oven of 375 degrees Fahrenheit (190 degrees Celsius). Take a bowl and stir together chopped garlic, vegetable oil, black pepper, lemon juice, salt, lemon zest, and dried dill.
2. Place the salmon pieces in just one column on a sheet with baking parchment. Employ a brush to spread the lemon-dill mixture on both sides of the salmon pieces.
3. Bake the salmon in an oven that has been warmed for approximately 15 to 20 minutes, so that it can be simply flaked with a fork.
4. Serve.

78. Baked Chicken Thighs with Garlic and Herbs

What we need:
- 2 tablespoons of vegetable oil
- 4 chicken thighs
- 4 cloves of cloves of garlic, crushed
- 1 teaspoon of teaspoon of teaspoon of thyme
- 1 teaspoon rosemary
- Salt and black pepper, to taste
- Fresh parsley, for garnish

Getting ready:
1. Put your oven at 375°F (190°C) to get it ready.
2. Mix the oil, thyme, salt, black pepper, garlic, and rosemary in a small bowl. Put the chicken legs on parchment paper on a baking sheet.
3. Brush the cloves and herb mixture on the chicken legs, making sure to cover them evenly. Bake it in an oven that has already been hot for 30 to 35 minutes, after which the chicken is done and the skin is crunchy.
4. If preferred, garnish with fresh parsley before serving.

79. Eggplant Lasagna

What we need:
- 1 cup of cup of cheese
- 1 large eggplant, sliced
- 1 pound of pound of crushed beef
- 1 can (14 ounces) of crushed tomatoes
- 3 cloves of cloves of garlic, chopped
- 1teaspoon of teaspoon of oregano
- black pepper and, Salt to taste
- Fresh basil leaves, for garnish (optional)

Getting ready:
1. Cook the seasoned meat in a pan that has been heated to medium-high heat.
2. Add the tomatoes, basil, oregano, garlic, black pepper, and salt to the pan. Simmer for around 10 minutes to create a flavorful sauce.
3. In another bowl, combine the chopped Parmesan, Ricotta, and mozzarella cheeses.
4. Stack the eggplant strips, meat sauce, and cheese mixture in a baking dish to make lasagna.
5. Continue layering until you've used all of your components, and then top with a cheese layer.

6. Roast in a warm oven for 28-35 minutes, so that the cheddar cheese is creamy and golden.
7. Embellish with fresh basil leaves before serving, if desired.

80. Spaghetti squash with pesto and cherry tomatoes

What we need:
- 1 medium-sized spaghetti squash
- 1 cup cherry tomatoes, halved
- ¼ cup prepared pesto sauce
- ¼ cup grated cheese
- Black pepper and salt, to taste
- For decorate Fresh basil leaves

Getting ready:
1. Heat your cooker and split your spaghetti vegetable in the heated oily center.
2. Put the cut side down of the squash halves on an oven rack lined with baking parchment.
3. To make "spaghetti" strands, roast the squash in a preheated oven for 35 to 40 minutes, or until it's tender.
4. Scoop up the spaghetti squash with a fork and place it in a serving dish.
5. Combine the cooked spaghetti squash with the cheese, pesto sauce, black pepper, and halved cherry tomatoes.
6. Beautify with fresh basil leaves before serving, if desired.

81. Lemon, garlic, shrimp, and asparagus

What we need:
- 1 pound of large shrimp washed
- 1 bunch of fresh, trimmed asparagus
- 4 minced garlic cloves
- 2 tablespoons of oil
- Salt and black pepper, to taste
- Parsley, to decorate

Getting ready:
1. Put the shrimp that have been peeled and deveined, asparagus that has been cut and trimmed, chopped garlic, salt, lemon juice, vegetable oil, lemon zest, and black pepper in a large dish. Mix it up to cover everything.
2. Put a big pan over low to medium heat to warm up. Place the shrimp and broccoli in the pan.

3. Cook for approximately 4 to 5 minutes, stirring every so often, as soon as the shrimp turns pinkish and opaque and the asparagus is tender-crisp.
4. Optional: Top with chopped fresh parsley just before serving.

82. Stuffed bell peppers

What we need:
- 5 large bell peppers, any color
- 1 pound of small cubed beef
- 1 cup of cauliflower rice
- 1 cup chopped tomatoes
- ½ cup finely chopped onion
- 3 crushed cloves garlic
- 1 teaspoon of oregano
- Salt and black pepper, to taste
- Shredded cheese, for topping

Getting ready:
1. To prepare your oven, heat it to 375 degrees Fahrenheit (190 degrees Celsius).
2. Slice the bell peppers into a tiny piece off the bottom to make a flat surface.
3. Brown the ground meat (or turkey) in a cooker on high heat. Mix the onion and garlic in the cooker. Fry the onion for a few minutes, as soon as it turns golden.
4. Mix in the rice cauliflower, tomatoes, salt, oregano, and black pepper. Keep cooking for 5 minutes more, so that the blend is fully warm.
5. Stuff the bell peppers that have been ready with the mixture of ground beef and broccoli rice. If you want, you can sprinkle chopped cheddar cheese on top of each stuffed pepper.
6. Put the bell peppers that have been stuffed in a dish for baking and cover them with aluminum foil. Bake it roughly 25–30 minutes in an oven that has already been warm, or till the peppers are soft.

83. Grilled Cilantro Lime Chicken

What we need:
For the Cilantro Lime Chicken:
- minced 2 cloves garlic
- 5 boneless breasts of chicken
- 2 tablespoons of vegetable oil
- 1 tsp. grated cumin
- Paprika ½ teaspoon

- pepper to taste
- Zest and juice of 2 limes
- Salt as need

For the Avocado Salsa:
- 2 avocados, diced
- 1 cup diced tomatoes
- ¼ cup finely diced fresh cilantro
- ¼ cup diced onion
- Juice of 1 lime
- Salt to taste
- Black pepper to taste

Getting ready:
1. Mix the vegetable oil, chopped garlic, cumin powder, and spice, and the lime zest, juice of the lime, salt, and black pepper in a bowl. Blend together for the sauce.
2. Coat the chicken breasts with the marinade and place them in a zipper-top bag or a small dish. Close the bag or dish and put it in the fridge for a minimum of 30 minutes.
3. Flame your grill to a moderately high temperature.
4. Grill the chicken breasts that have been marinating for about 6 to 7 minutes per side, so that they are fully cooked and have grill lines.
5. Make the avocado salsa by mixing diced avocados, tomatoes, chopped cilantro, diced onion, chopped lime juice, salt, and black pepper in a separate bowl.
6. Put a big scoop of avocado salsa on top of the grilled cilantro lime chicken.

84. Lamb with asparagus

What we need:
- 3-pound bone-in leg of lamb
- 5 cups of fresh asparagus
- Three minced garlic cloves
- 12 tsp. dried thyme
- 1/4 cups of fresh, chopped mint
- ¼ cup of water
- Two tablespoons of grass-fed butter
- ½ tsp. dried parsley
- Pepper and salt as needed.

Getting ready:
1. Once it has been dried, the lamb should be rubbed all over with a combination that includes salt, thyme, parsley, and pepper.

2. To make the butter easier to work with, microwave it in a big dish.
3. Include lamb and cook it for around five minute's total, cooking it on both sides.
4. Put the lamb on top of the element that is heating up the oven.
5. Garlic and mint should be added, depending on the situation.
6. Pour in water.
7. At a relatively close distance to the cover of the pan.
8. Ten hours of preparation should be done on a low------heat setting. After the allotted amount of time has passed, remove the lamb from the oven and place it in a separate location.
9. After putting the lamb back on the surface of the vegetables in the cooker, which was the last step, add the asparagus.
10. Next to the cover of the pot, and then continue to let it simmer for another two hours after that.
11. Serve!

85. Zoodles with meatballs in an Italian sauce

What we need:
- 1 medium twisted zucchini
- 2 cups beef stock
- 1 tablespoon of sliced onion 2 ribs of chopped celery
- 1 carrot that's been chopped
- 1 tomato, medium-sized, diced;
- 6 cloves of garlic, crushed
- 1 ½ pound ground beef
- 1 ½ t. garlic salt
- ½ and a half cups of shredded parmesan cheese
- 1 big egg
- ½ teaspoon black pepper
- 4 tablespoons of finely minced fresh parsley
- Dry minced onions
- Himalayan pink salt
- 1 tablespoon of each
- Italian spice, dried oregano Italian seasoning

Getting ready:
1. Turn on the cooker and put it in a low temperature situation.
2. Put the carrot, zucchini, onion, celery, tomato, garlic salt, and beef stock into the slow cooker. Put the cap back on.

3. In a bowl or other container, combine the ground beef, parmesan, parsley, Italian spices, egg, pepper, sea salt, oregano, garlic paste, and onion powder. Combine, and then roll into thirty golf-ball-sized meatballs.
4. In a cooker set on high-medium heat, bring the oil up to temperature. When it is heated, add the meatballs that have been browned and throw them into the slow cooker.
5. Prepare on a low setting while keeping the lid on for a period of six hours.

86. Curried cauliflower soup

What we need:
- 3 cups of water
- One small cauliflower
- Unsalted butter (one teaspoon)
- One onion, chopped
- Sour cream (½ cup)
- Curry powder (two teaspoons)
- Garlic, minced (2 teaspoons)
- Cilantro, chopped

Getting ready:
1. Utilizing a big pan and heating it over a moderate setting will ensure that the butter is thoroughly melted.
2. Cooking the onion and garlic for around three minutes should be sufficient time.
3. The cauliflower, curry powder, and water should all be mixed together in a big bowl.
4. After the ingredients have reached a rolling boil, lower the heat to a slow boil.
5. Maintain a low simmer for around twenty minutes.
6. Place the elements in a food processor and blend them until the result is as pulpy and creamy as silk.
7. Repeat the process of transferring the soup to the saucepan.
8. Mix in the finely chopped coriander as well as the sour cream.

87. Shrimp Gravy

What we need:
- 3 pieces of bacon in strips
- 2 tablespoons of ghee or margarine that has not been salted
- 1 green ringer pepper, slashed
- ½ cup of onions cut into dice
- 1 clove of garlic, either finely chopped or pulverized to a paste.
- 1 pound of huge shrimp, peeled and deveined, numbering maybe about 30

- 2 tablespoons of fine-grained salt from the ocean
- ½ tablespoons of dark pepper that has been ground
- ½ cup of chicken bone stock

Getting ready:
1. Over medium-high heat, cook the bacon in a cast iron pan for about 4 minutes, so that it is crispy. Remove it from the pan and set it aside in a secure location. Keep the fat in the pan so that you can use it later.
2. After putting the ghee in the pan with the bacon grease, turn the heat down to medium. Add the onions and bell pepper to the pan, and then cook everything for about five minutes, so that the onions are soft. After a minute or two, add the garlic and continue cooking.
3. The shrimp should be seasoned with salt and pepper. After putting the shrimp in the pan, turn the heat up to medium-high and continue sautéing while constantly mixing the ingredients for approximately four minutes, up to when the shrimp are brown and no longer see-through. The shrimp should be put on a hot plate using a spoon with an open end, and then put in a safe place.
4. While maintaining the medium-high heat, decant the stock into the pan and utilize a whisk to work it into the base of the pan to deglaze it. At this time, take out the pan from the flare, mix the shrimp with the sauce, and stir to coat.

88. Cauliflower Rice and Luau Pork

What we need:
- 1 cup Pork
- Roast pork weighing three pounds
- 1.5 grams of traditional table salt
- Two teaspoons of the liquid from the hickory
- Four individual pieces of bacon
- Five individual cloves of garlic
- Cauliflower is equivalent to three cups of it.
- A quarter of a teaspoon's worth of garlic paste
- 2 teaspoons of chicken stock 0.25 of a teaspoon of salt

Getting ready:
1. When you are finished arranging the bacon on the inside of the cooker, sprinkle the garlic cloves in an equal coating over the top of it.
2. After it has been prepared, the roast should be seasoned before being put in the slow cooker.
3. It is necessary to include the hickory liquid in the combination.

4. After spending the first six hours of the entire cooking period with the heat turned up high, reduce it to a low setting for the last two hours of the procedure.
5. It is strongly suggested that the cauliflower be steamed.
6. Include them in the mixture that is now being reduced to a powder in the food processor.
7. It is appropriate to serve both at the same time.

89. Roasted-beef Stew

What we need:
- Flour (¼ cup)
- Garlic (2 teaspoons)
- Thyme (1 teaspoon)
- Vegetable oil
- One carrot
- ½ sweet onion, chopped
- Water
- Beef stock, prepared (1 cup)
- 2 celery stalks
- Beef chuck roast, boneless (½ pound)
- 1 teaspoon cornstarch
- Grated black pepper
- 2 tablespoons parsley, chopped

Getting ready:
1. Preheat your oven (350°F). Place the black pepper and flour in a big synthetic freezer bag; toss well.
2. Combine the beef pieces in the bag and swirl to coat. Heat the ovenproof pot with vegetable oil.
3. Bake the beef pieces for a few minutes, so that they become brown. Eliminate the beef; set it aside on a platter.
4. After adding the garlic and onion to the saucepan, let them simmer for around three minutes. As you deglaze the saucepan and remove any leftovers from the bottom, place them in the beef stock.
5. Put some water, carrots, celery, beef drippings, and thyme on a plate. Put the pan in the stove and lock the lid on tight.
6. Bake the stew, occasionally stirring, for around 1 hour. Take the stew from the cooker.
7. Add cornstarch and 2 tsp. of water and stir them into the hot stew to thicken the sauce. Season them with black pepper. Serve them with parsley.

90. Chicken Noodle Soup

What we need:
- Chicken broth (1 ½ cups)
- Salt
- Cooked chicken (1 cup)
- Water
- Black pepper
- Carrot (¼ cup)
- Poultry seasoning (¼ tsp)
- Uncooked egg noodles (2 oz.)

Getting ready:
1. Place the broth and water in your slow cooker. Add the pepper, salt, and poultry seasoning to them.
2. Chop the carrot and strip the chicken. Add them to the noodles and soup.
3. Cook them for around 25 minutes. When it is done, it serves after chilling for a few moments.

91. Baked Cod with Lemon and Herbs

What we need:
- 4 cod fillets
- Sap and zest of 1 lemon
- 3 cloves of garlic, crushed
- 2 tablespoons of vegetable oil
- 1 teaspoon dry parsley
- 1 teaspoon dried dill
- Salt to taste
- Fresh dill to decorate
- Black pepper to taste

Getting ready:
1. Set your oven to 190 degrees Celsius.
2. Take a large dish and mix all the elements—lemon zest, lemon sap, vegetable oil, crushed garlic, black pepper, salt, parsley, and dill—to create a marinade.
3. Place the cod fillets in a roasting cooker.
4. Marinate the cod fillets by pouring the marinade over them and turning them over a few times to ensure uniform coverage.
5. Bake the fish in an oven that has been warmed for approximately 15–20 minutes, so that it can be easily flaked apart with a fork.

6. Dress up with fresh dill before serving, if desired.

92. Lemon Herb Grilled Chicken Breast

What we need:
- Zest and sap of 2 lemons
- 5 boneless, skinless chicken breasts
- 2 cloves of garlic, crushed
- 2 tablespoons of vegetable oil
- 1 teaspoon of oregano
- 1 teaspoon dehydrated thyme
- As tasted, salt and black pepper
- Fresh parsley, for decoration

Getting ready:
1. To make the marinade, place the lime zest, the juice of a lemon, chopped garlic, dried oregano, baked thyme, minced garlic, vegetable oil, and a pinch each of pepper and salt in a bowl.
2. Cover the chicken breasts with the marinade and put them in a shallow dish or a container with a zip-top cover. Make sure the dish or bag is covered and refrigerated for a minimum of thirty minutes.
3. Increase the grill's temperature to a medium-high.
4. The chicken breasts should be grilled for 6 to 7 minutes per side after marinating, or until cooked through and barbecue marks appear.
5. If wanted, garnish the dish with fresh parsley just before serving.

93. Spicy Cauliflower Rice with Ground Turkey

What we need:
- 1 pound of ground turkey
- 4 cups cauliflower rice
- 1 bell pepper, diced
- minced 2 cloves of garlic
- 1 teaspoon chili red chili flakes
- ½ cup diced onion
- 3 tablespoons of vegetable oil
- ½ teaspoon cumin
- To taste, black pepper and salt
- Fresh cilantro, for decoration

Getting ready:

1. Place the vegetable oil in a pan over high heat and bring it to a boil.
2. To the pan, add the garlic that has been minced and the onions that have been diced. Sauté the onions for a few minutes, so that they turn translucent, and then remove from the heat.
3. Mix crushed turkey into the pan already in use. Cook it until it has a browned appearance and is done all the way through, breaking it up with a spoon as you go.
4. After adding the bell pepper that has been chopped and sliced in its entirety to the pan, continue to boil the mixture for an additional two to three minutes so that the pepper may begin to become tenderer.
5. Chili powder, cumin, cayenne pepper, salt, and black pepper are the following ingredients that should be added to the turkey mixture before it is seasoned.
6. Give everything a thorough mixing so that all of the spices are dispersed evenly.
7. To prepare the cauliflower rice, add it to the pan and stir-fry it for around five to seven minutes. During this time, you should wait for it to be cooked and fully absorb the flavors.
8. Give the ingredients a taste and make any necessary adjustments, such as adding additional salt, pepper, or cayenne pepper.
9. Serve your spicy cauliflower rice with ground turkey hot, garnished with fresh cilantro if you like.

SNACKS

94. Guacamole-stuffed cucumber bites

What we need:
- 2 cucumbers
- 2 ripe avocados
- 1 small, diced tomato
- ¼ cup finely chopped onion
- 2 tablespoons chopped fresh cilantro
- Juice of 1 lime
- Red pepper flakes
- To taste salt and black pepper

Getting ready:
1. Slice the cucumbers into thin rounds, and then remove the seeds from each round using a melon baller or a small spoon. This should leave a tiny well in the center of each round of cucumber. Put them to the side.
2. Mash the ripe avocados in a basin till they reach a creamy consistency.

3. To the mashed avocado, add the diced tomato, the finely diced red onion, the chopped cilantro, the lime juice and salt, black pepper, and the flakes of red pepper (if preferred). Guacamole may be made by combining all of the ingredients in a mixing bowl.
4. Fill each cucumber round with a spoonful of guacamole.
5. Arrange the guacamole-stuffed cucumber bites on a serving platter.
6. Serve and enjoy these refreshing snacks!

95. Caprese Skewers with a Balsamic Glaze

What we need:
- Wooden skewers
- 20 fresh mozzarella cheese balls
- 20 cherry tomatoes
- 20 fresh basil leaves
- Balsamic glaze (approximately 1/4 cup)

Getting ready:
1. Assemble your Caprese Skewers by threading a cherry tomato, a fresh cheese ball, and a single leaf of fresh basil on each skewer made of wood.
2. Put the skewers on a plate to serve.
3. Drizzle balsamic glaze over the skewers just before serving.
4. These Caprese Skewers make for a delightful and visually appealing snack.

96. Cucumber and Cream Cheese Roll-Ups

What we need:
- black pepper and Salt, to taste
- 1 cucumber
- 4 ounces cheese
- Garlic Paste
- ¼ cup diced onion
- garlic paste ¼ teaspoon

Getting ready:
1. Using a vegetable peeler or a mandolin-style slicer, cut the cucumber into long, thin slices lengthwise.
2. Take a large dish; whisk the cheese that has been melted, the chopped yellow and green bell peppers, the chopped red onion, the crushed garlic, the salt, and the black pepper until everything is well blended.
3. Arrange a cucumber strip on the surface, and then top it with a very thin coating of the cream cheese mixture.

4. Wrap the cucumber strip in a crescent roll with the cream cheese filling inside.
5. Proceed in the same manner with the rest of the cucumber slices.
6. Arrange the cucumber and cream cheese roll-ups on a serving platter.
7. Chill for a bit before serving for a refreshing and snack.

97. Greek Yogurt with Berries and Almonds

What we need:
- 2 cups Greek yogurt (unsweetened)
- ½ cup mixed berries
- 3 tablespoons of sliced almonds
- 1 teaspoon of honey
- Mint leaves to decorate

Getting ready:
1. In a serving bowl, scoop the Greek yogurt.
2. Various berries and sliced almonds make a tasty topping for yogurt.
3. Optionally, sprinkle honey over the top for a touch of sweetness.
4. Garnish with fresh mint leaves, if desired.
5. This yogurt among almonds and berries is a creamy, fruity, and satisfying snack.

98. Parmesan Zucchini Crisps

What we need:
- 2 medium-sized zucchinis
- ½ teaspoon garlic paste
- ½ cup grated cheese
- ¼ cup almond flour
- To taste salt and black pepper,
- 1 egg, flattened

Getting ready:
1. Prepare your oven by preheating it. Use parchment paper to line a baking sheet.
2. The zucchinis should be sliced into thin rounds.
3. Take a bowl; combine the grated cheese, garlic paste, almond flour, black pepper, salt, and dried oregano.
4. Once every zucchini round has been dipped into the beaten egg and any excess removed, cover it with a mixture of bread crumbs and Parmesan cheese.
5. Place the covered zucchini rounds on the organized roasting sheet.
6. Roast the zucchini crisps in an oven that has been warmed for approximately 15 to 20 minutes, so that they have a golden color and a crispy texture.

7. Before serving, remove them from the preheated oven and let them cool somewhat. Crumbs.
8. These Parmesan Zucchini Crisps are a crunchy and savory snack.

99. Deviled Eggs with Bacon

What we need:
- 6 hard-boiled eggs, peeled and halved
- 3 tablespoons of mayonnaise
- 2 teaspoons Dijon mustard
- 2 strips of cooked bacon, crumbled
- 1 teaspoon chopped fresh chives
- To taste salt and black pepper
- Smoked paprika

Getting ready:
1. Cut the eggs that have been hard-boiled in half lengthwise, and then softly take away the yolks from all sides.
2. Take a dish and mash the egg yolks with mayonnaise, Dijon mustard, crumbled bacon, salt, chopped chives, and black pepper until smooth.
3. Split the egg whites in half and spoon some of the yolk mixture into each half.
4. A dash of smoked paprika is an optional garnish.
5. Arrange the deviled eggs with bacon on a serving platter.
6. Enjoy these flavorful and protein-packed snacks!

100. Smoked Salmon with Cucumber

What we need:
- 1 cucumber
- 4 ounces of fried salmon
- 4 tablespoons of cream cheese
- Fresh dill to decorate
- Lemon zest

Getting ready:
1. Slice the cucumber into thick rounds.
2. Apply a smear of mozzarella in a thin layer over every cucumber that is round.
3. Apex each cucumber round with a piece of fried salmon.
4. Garnish with fresh dill if desired.
5. Serve with lemon zest on the part for an extra zesty touch.

101. Almond and Coconut Energy Bites

What we need:

- ¼ cup flour of almond
- 1 cup butter of almond
- ½ cup shredded coconut
- ½ cup chia seeds
- ¼ cup chocolate chips
- 2 tablespoons of sweetener (e.g., erythritol or stevia)
- 1 teaspoon of vanilla essence
- Salt

Getting ready:

1. In a mixing bowl, combine almond butter, shredded coconut, almond flour, chia seeds, sugar-free chocolate chips, sweetener, vanilla essence, and salt.
2. Combine until all the elements are nicely mixed.
3. Using your hands, roll the mixture into little balls that are suitable for snacking.
4. Arrange the energy bites in a single layer on a sheet coated with baking parchment, and place the tray in the fridge to chill for approximately half an hour.
5. To make this a delightful snack that is ready in a flash; keep it in the fridge in an airtight box.

102. Spicy Roasted Chickpeas

What we need:

- 3 tablespoons of vegetable oil
- 1 cup of chickpeas
- smoked paprika 2 teaspoons
- ½ teaspoon chili flakes
- ½ teaspoon crushed garlic
- ½ teaspoon grated cumin
- Grated pepper and salt

Getting ready:

1. Set the cooker to 200 degrees Celsius.
2. After rinsing and draining the chickpeas, blot them thoroughly with a paper towel and keep them sideways.
3. Put the beans Take a bowl; and then add the vegetable oil, smoked paprika, chili flakes, crushed garlic, salt, cumin, and black pepper. Toss the chickpeas to the point they are equally covered with the vegetable oil mixture.
4. Arrange the chickpeas on a baking sheet so that they form one layer.

5. Put them in an oven that has been warmed and roast them for approximately 25–30 minutes, tossing them once or twice during that time, as long as they are crispy.
6. Let the spicy roasted chickpeas cool before enjoying this crunchy and savory snack.

103. Mini Bell Pepper Nachos

What we need:
- Mini bell peppers
- ½ cup cubed beef seasoning as tacos
- ½ cup shredded cheddar cheese
- Sliced jalapeños (optional)
- Guacamole, salsa, or sour cream for dipping (optional)

Getting ready:
1. Remove the seeds and slice the mini bell peppers in half.
2. Fill each bell pepper half with a spoonful of cooked ground beef or turkey.
3. Before serving, top with shredded cheddar cheese.S
4. If you like it spicy, add sliced jalapeños.
5. Arrange the Mini Bell Pepper Nachos on a baking sheet.
6. Turn the oven on high and bake the shredded cheese for two minutes, so that it becomes soft and bubbling.
7. Enjoy with guacamole, salsa, or sour cream for dipping, if desired.

104. Cauliflower Buffalo Bites

What we need:
- 1 cauliflower head, chop into bite-sized florets, and set aside.
- ½ cup flour
- ½ cup almond milk
- ¼ cup hot sauce (adjust to your preferred level of spiciness)
- garlic paste 1 teaspoon
- To taste black pepper and salt
- Blue cheese for dressing

Getting ready:
1. Prepare your oven with a baking sheet and baking parchment.
2. To make the batter, put the almond flour, almond milk, spicy sauce, garlic paste, some salt, and some black pepper into a bowl.
3. After dipping each cauliflower floret into the batter and ensuring that it is evenly coated, place it on the baking sheet.

4. Place the cauliflower in an oven that has been warmed and roast for approximately 20 to 25 minutes, turning it over halfway through the cooking process, until it is golden and crispy brown.
5. If you choose, you can serve your Buffalo Cauliflower Chips with blue cheese ranch or ranch dressing on the side for dipping.

105. Crispy Cheese

What we need:
- 1 cup shredded cheese (or your preferred cheese)
- ¼ teaspoon paprika
- ¼ teaspoon garlic paste
- ¼ teaspoon dried herbs

Getting ready:
1. Prepare a temperature in your oven of 375 degrees Fahrenheit (190 degrees Celsius). A baking dish should be lined with baking parchment.
2. Take a bowl and mix shredded cheddar cheese with any optional seasonings you like (paprika, garlic paste, dried herbs).
3. Divide the cheese mixture into little mounds and place them spaced apart on the parchment paper.
4. Using the back of a spoon, gently press each mound into a little flatter shape.
5. Place the cheese crisps in an oven that has been prepared and bake for approximately 5-7 minutes, until they are golden brown and bubbling.
6. When you are ready to eat these crispy keto cheese crisps, extract them from the heated oven and allow them to cool for a few minutes.

106. Meatballs

What we need:
- 1 kg of beef that was raised on grass
- A total of four cups of beef stock
- The equivalent of four tablespoons of sugar-free tomato paste
- Cumin to the tune of two tablespoons
- Seasoning with two tablespoons of Italian oregano
- Paprika, to taste, two tablespoons
- As required, pepper and salt may be used.

Getting ready:
1. Mix the meat with the spices, and then roll the mixture into balls.
2. Place it in the slow cooker you have.

3. Combine the stock and tomato paste in a blender until it is completely smooth.
4. Move the meatballs to the pan where they will cook.
5. Within close proximity to the lid of the pan.
6. Putting it in the oven at a high temperature for a period of two hours
7. Please serve it hot!

107. Sweet and spicy shrimp

What we need:
- Two kilograms of raw prawns, which have been de-wrapped and cleaned
- 3/4 cup vegetable oil
- A little amount of dried chili flakes
- Stevia in liquid form, four tablespoons' worth
- One teaspoon of sweet paprika
- Sriracha to taste, two tablespoons
- As required, pepper and salt may be used.

Getting ready:
1. Mix vegetable oil, stevia, Sriracha, chili flakes, paprika, pepper, and a pinch of salt in a pan.
2. Within close proximity to the lid of the pan.
3. Putting it through the oven at a high temperature for half an hour.
4. Taste the sauce and adjust the amount of sweetness and spice to suit your preferences.
5. After adding the raw shrimp, whisk the mixture to coat it.
6. Within close proximity to the lid of the pan.
7. Putting it through a high-temperature cooking process for ten minutes.
8. Serve!

108. Cheesy spaghetti squash

What we need:
- One large spaghetti squash, which weighs about 5 pounds
- 3/4 cup shredded mozzarella
- Cottage cheese equaling 5 ounces
- ¼ cup of parsley that has been chopped
- 14 cups of butter from grass-fed cows
- 1 ounce and 5 ounces of grated Parmesan cheese
- Two cloves of garlic that have been minced
- Pepper and salt

Getting ready:
1. Cut your squash in half lengthwise, cutting it part by part.
2. Place it in the slow cooker with the cut side facing down, right next to the lid of the pan.
3. Prepare it by cooking it at a high temperature for two to three hours.
4. Delicately remove the squash from the oven once the timer goes off.
5. Put the butter and garlic in the pan so that they may melt.
6. Remove the seeds from the cooked squash while protecting your hands with oven mitts.
7. After using a fork to separate the flesh from the bones, return to the kitchen to finish preparing the meal.
8. Combine the cottage cheese with the parmesan cheese in a mixing bowl.
9. Add a little pepper and salt to taste.
10. After that, give it a thorough whisk.
11. Mozzarella should be sprinkled on top, and then the dish should be moved close to the lid of the slow cooker so that any additional heat may melt the cheese.
12. Before digging in, sprinkle with minced parsley.

109. Prosciutto-Garlic Green Beans

What we need:
- 5 kg of freshly picked green beans
- 4-ounces prosciutto
- Ten cloves of garlic that have been minced
- A third of a cup of brown sugar substitute called Sukrin Gold.
- Just enough water to cover the beans Move the dough carefully onto the parchment paper
- ½ cup of butter from grass-fed cows
- To enhance the flavor, pepper and salt were added.

Getting ready:
1. Throw everything into the pot or the cooker.
2. After cooking it at a high temperature for one hour, reduce it to a low temperature for four hours.
3. After that, give it a taste, and if you think it needs more salt or pepper, add some more of those seasonings.

110. Fresh veggies with herbs

What we need:
- 2 and a half cups of sliced zucchini
- Two coffee glasses filled with yellow bell peppers
- A couple of cups of crisp spinach
- 1 ½ cups sweet onion
- One and a half cups of grape tomatoes
- There is ½ cup of vegetable oil.
- ½ espresso cup worth of balsamic vinegar
- Two teaspoons of freshly chopped basil
- One tablespoon of fresh thyme that has been chopped

Getting ready:
1. In a large basin, toss all the vegetables together.
2. Blend the balsamic vinegar and vegetable oil together in a separate container to make an emulsion.
3. Mix the herbs into the basin containing the dressing.
4. Place the vegetables inside the slow cooker.
5. Mix the salad with dressing, cover the pan, and let it set for a few minutes.
6. It should be cooked at a low temperature for three hours, with stirring taking place every hour.
7. Serve!

111. Veggie Stir-Fry

What we need:
- Mixed fresh vegetables, sliced or julienned, such as carrots mushrooms, burst peas, broccoli florets, and bell peppers
- Aromatics, such as garlic and ginger, are finely chopped.
- The protein of your choosing, such as tofu or temper, cubed or scored
- Boiling oil of your choice, such as sesame oil or vegetable oil
- Stir-fry the spice of your choice, such as soy sauce or teriyaki sauce.
- Cooked rice or noodles

Getting ready:
1. Take a big pot and heat a teaspoon of oil or butter until it sizzles.
2. Count the crushed garlic and ginger in heated oil to show their aromatic dance and taste base.
3. Toss the sliced or julienned veggies into the stir-fry, visualizing their vivid colors and pleasant crunch.

4. Stir-fry the veggies quickly, relishing the sizzling noises and tender-crisp texture.
5. Sprinkle the stir-fry sauce over the veggies and toss to evenly cover.
6. Stir-fry for a few more minutes to absorb spices and solidify the sauce.
7. Take the wok off the burner and admire the colorful veggies and wonderful perfume.
8. Enjoy the veggie stir-fry over rice or noodles for extra flavor and heartiness.

112. Pizza Casserole

What we need:
- 2 boneless chicken breasts in the package
- 2 whole cloves of garlic
- 1 level teaspoon of spice, a dash of Italian pepper
- Eight fluid ounces of tomato paste
- 1 piece of fresh mozzarella half a cup 1 bay leaf, 0.25 tablespoons of salt

Getting ready:
1. In the slow cooker, place the chicken.
2. Mix in the other ingredients, except the cheese.
3. Bake on low heat for four hours.
4. When the cooking is finished, sprinkle some cheese on top.

113. Sweet and spicy Thai pizza

What you need:
- 1 cup of boiling water
- 1 tablespoon of sugar
- 1 teaspoon salt
- 1 tablespoon sesame oil
- 2 ½ cups all-purpose flour
- 1 cup Thai sauce (store-bought or homemade)
- 1 cup chopped raw peanuts
- 1 tablespoon Thai basil leaves
- 1 cup mozzarella cheese

Getting ready:
1. In a mixing dish, add the warm water, sugar, and yeast. Wait 5–10 minutes, so that the mixture turns frothy, before using. Then, whisk in the salt and sesame oil. The flour should be added slowly while mixing to ensure cohesive dough.
2. Knead the dough on an area of flour for 5 to 7 minutes, so it is smooth and elastic. Dough should be allowed to rise in an oiled basin covered with a moist towel for 1 to 2 hours before it has doubled in size.

3. Set the temperature of the oven to 245°C and put a pizza plate lined with parchment paper inside to heat up. On a clean surface, spread out the dough to the size and form you want. Carefully place the dough on top of the parchment paper.
4. Apply Thai sauce evenly over pizza dough, leaving a tiny margin on the edges. Use the paper towel to delicately transfer the pizza to the cooked platter.
5. Bake for about ten to ½ minutes so that the loaf is brown and the cream cheese has softened and is lightly browning. After removing the pizza from the oven, let it aside for a few minutes to cool.
6. Finally, top the sweet and spicy Thai-inspired pizza with fresh cilantro leaves, chopped raw peanuts, and Thai basil leaves for a burst of flavor and texture. Enjoy your homemade Thai-inspired pizza creation!

114. Pancakes

What we need:
- 2 eggs
- 2 ounces of softened cheese cream
- ½ teaspoon vanilla essence
- 2 tablespoons of almond flour
- ½ teaspoon baking powder
- A little of salt
- Sweetener
- Butter or coconut oil for cooking

Getting ready:
1. Ensure that your cream cheese is softened and that you have all the necessary elements at hand.
2. Take a mixer and blend the eggs, baking powder, softened cream cheese, almond flour, vanilla essence, and a little salt. Here is where you can add your preferred sweetener if you want your pancakes on the sweet side. Mix together, awaiting the mixture to be well combined and smooth. If you allow the batter a few minutes to settle, you will notice that it becomes somewhat thicker.
3. Prepare a griddle or a skillet by heating it over a low to medium flame. To prevent sticking, mix in a tiny bit of coconut oil.
4. You can produce pancakes of whatever size you choose by dropping spoonfuls of batter onto the heated griddle in the appropriate amounts. Make use of the back of a spoon to spread the batter out into the form you want it to take. Bring the liquid to a boil and continue to do so for approximately two to three minutes so that the surfaces of the liquid begin to show signs of bubble formation.

5. Pancakes should be delicately flipped using a spatula once bubbles appear and edges begin to harden. Fry the second side for a further two minutes, so that they are golden brown all the way through and completely done.
6. Take the pancakes out of the skillet and put them on a serving dish. They are best enjoyed hot. You can top them with ingredients such as sugar-free syrup, fresh berries, whipped cream (unsweetened), or a dollop of sugar-free nut butter.
7. If you want to add an extra coat of texture and flavor, consider garnishing your pancakes with chopped almonds, chia seeds, or a sprinkle of unsweetened cocoa powder.
8. Continue making pancakes with the remaining batter until it's all used up. This recipe typically yields 2-4 pancakes, depending on the size.

115. Twist Pizza

What you need:
- 1 lb. cubed beef
- 1 small onion, chopped very small
- 1 cup of fresh corn kernels
- 2 chopped garlic cloves
- Add salt and black pepper.
- 1 packet of spice mix for tacos
- ½ cup of liquid
- 1 cup of drained and washed black beans from a can
- 1 cup diced bell pepper

Getting ready:
1. Add sliced beef to a large pan over high heat and cook until crumbly, mashing with a fork. Mix the onion and crushed garlic in the pan after two to three minutes and boil until translucent.
2. Stir in the taco spice mix and the water, and let the combination boil for two to three minutes so that it thickens. Mix the corn, small tomatoes, black beans, and bell peppers. Cook the vegetables for another 5–7 minutes, so that they are softened. Salt and black pepper are optional seasonings. Take it off the heat and put it sideways.
3. Place a few pieces of the chopped cheese in the bottom of each tortilla dish. Fry in an oven that is preheated to warm for five to seven minutes, so that the tortillas have become crisp and the cheese has melted and is bubbling. Put a big scoop of the taco filling mixture into each crispy tortilla bowl.
4. Add some chopped lettuce, diced avocado, and sour cream on top. For an extra kick, drizzle salsa or hot sauce over the top and sprinkle with fresh cilantro.

5. Put each Taco Tuesday Twist bowl on a separate plate and serve right away while they are still hot and tasty. Every bite of this unique take on classic tacos is something to enjoy.

116. Diavola Pizza

What you need:
- 200 ml of yeast for making beer
- 12 loaves of bread
- 2 tablespoons of vegetable oil
- 1 pinch of salt
- 400 grams of flour
- For the sauce,
- Original vegetable oil
- Oregano to taste Salt to taste
- 150 g of ham with a kick
- 250 grams of mozzarella
- 400 grams of tomato sauce

Getting ready:
1. Start by making the dough for the pizza. Get a baking sheet and lubricate it with a drop or two of oil. After it has been rolled out, the dough should be placed on a baking pan. Apply some tomato paste on top of it, and then put it in the preheated oven.
2. Slice the salami thinly, and cut the mozzarella into little cubes. Take the pizza out of the oven and evenly place the salami and cheese on it.
3. Add a little salt, a splash of oil, and a sprinkle of oregano, and roast for 20 more minutes to complete.

117. Vegan Pizza

What you need:
- 6 whole cherry tomatoes, chopped.
- Vegan mozzarella with a lower fat content
- 2 mushroom slices, cut
- Six tablespoons of tomato paste
- 1/4 of an onion, red, chopped
- Fresh basil that has been chopped
- Gluten-free pizza dough using just three ingredients
- A set of instructions

Getting ready:
1. Prepare an oven temperature of 400 degrees Fahrenheit (or around 200 degrees Celsius).
2. If you're going to use our gluten-free pizza dough made with only three ingredients, roast it for five minutes before continuing with the rest of the process.
3. If you are cooking using pizza dough that you purchased from a shop, be sure to follow the instructions on the packaging.
4. After removing the crust from the oven, put tomato paste, vegan mozzarella, mushrooms, and red onion in an equal coat above the apex of it.
5. Roast for a further five to ten minutes so that a golden brown color has been achieved.
6. Take the pizza out of the oven and spread it with tomatoes and basil before returning it to the oven.

118. Grilled Sandwich

What we need:
- Peanut butter (2 tbsp)
- Jelly (1 tbsp.)
- Two slices of white bread
- 2 tsp. unsalted butter

Getting ready:
1. Preheat your cooker.
2. Add the butter to the bread.
3. Expand the jelly and peanut butter on the unbuttered surfaces.
4. Set the sandwich together and put it in the pan.
5. Lightly brown them on all sides while grilling.

119. Mini Burger Sliders

What we need:
For the Mini Burger Patties:
- ½ pound cubed beef
- ½ teaspoon garlic paste
- Black pepper and salt to taste

For the burger toppings:
- Mini lettuce leaves
- Sliced cherry tomatoes
- Sliced dill pickles
- Mustard and sugar-free ketchup for dipping.

Getting ready:
1. Take a big dish and combine the cubed beef (or turkey), black pepper, garlic paste, and salt. Mix it up nicely.
2. Form the mixture into little patties the size of sliders.
3. Bake the tiny burger patties in a pan or skillet heated to medium-high heat for approximately two to three minutes on each side to ensure they achieve the amount of doneness you choose.
4. Assemble your Mini Burger Sliders by placing a patty on a lettuce leaf and adding sliced cherry tomatoes and pickles.
5. Serve with mustard and sugar-free ketchup for dipping.

120. Portobello Mushroom Burger Bites

What we need:
- black pepper and Salt
- Portobello mushroom caps (one for each bite)
- Ground beef (or ground turkey)
- Your choice of burger toppings (e.g., lettuce, tomato, cheese, onions)
- Vegetable oil

Getting ready:
1. Prepare your grill to 400 degrees Fahrenheit (200 degrees Celsius).
2. Remove the oyster mushroom caps' stems, and then lightly brush the caps with vegetable oil before putting them aside. To taste, add a little salt and freshly ground black pepper.
3. Bake the mushroom caps for about five minutes on each side, so that they become tender and slightly charred.
4. While the mushrooms are cooking, shape small burger patties from the ground beef (or turkey) and flavor them with black pepper and salt.
5. The little burger patties should be cooked on a grill or in a pan for approximately two to three minutes on each side so that they achieve the amount of doneness that you choose.
6. Assemble your Portobello Mushroom Burger Bites by placing a mini patty on top of a grilled mushroom cap and adding your choice of burger toppings.
7. Secure each bite with a toothpick.

121. Tacos

What we need:
- Large lettuce leaves
- Lean cubes of beef
- Your favorite burger toppings (e.g., sliced cheese, onions, tomatoes, pickles, avocado)
- Mustard, ketchup, or sugar-free BBQ sauce for drizzling

Getting ready:
1. In a skillet, boil the beef (or turkey) over a high-medium flame, breaking it apart into crumbles as it boils. Season it with black pepper and salt.
2. Once the meat is cooked, drain any excess grease.
3. Assemble your lettuce wrap burger "Tacos" by using large lettuce leaves as tacos. To assemble the burgers, stuff them with the meat that is cooked and a garnish of your choice.
4. Drizzle with mustard, ketchup, or sugar-free BBQ sauce for added flavor.
5. Fold the lettuce leaves around the filling to create a "taco"

122. Chicken and Vegetable Kabobs

What we need:
- Vegetable oil
- ½ medium onions
- Chopped thyme (½ teaspoon)
- Garlic, minced
- Pressed lemon juice (2 tablespoons)
- One summer squash
- Boneless chicken breast (4 ounces)

Getting ready:
1. Add the lemon juice, thyme, vegetable oil, and garlic to a dish and swirl well.
2. Next, add the chicken breast to the dish and fry well.
3. Put the dish in the refrigerator after covering it with a plastic cork and closing it.
4. After 1 hour, add the onion, chicken pieces, and squash to four large skewers, and distribute the vegetables and meat among the skewers.
5. Heat a barbecue and grill for around 12 minutes.

123. Roasted Pepper with Chicken

What we need:
- Garlic, minced (½ teaspoon)
- Vegetable oil
- French bread (4 slices)
- Chicken breast, cooked (4 ounces)
- One roasted red bell pepper
- Basil (½ cup)

Getting ready:
1. Pre-heat your oven.
2. Wrap a cooking sheet with foil made from aluminum and set it aside.
3. Take a small bowl and combine the garlic and vegetable oil in a way that is thorough.
4. Coat both sides of each slice of bread with a combination of vegetable oil and garlic.
5. Toast them for about five minutes on each side after placing them on the cooking pan.
6. Later, add the chicken, basil, and red pepper to a pot and stir well.
7. Garnish the top of every toasted bread wedge with the red pepper mixture.

124. Antojitos

What we need:
- Cream cheese (6 ounces)
- Ground coriander
- ½ jalapeño pepper, chopped
- Chili powder
- ½ scallion, chopped
- Red bell pepper, chopped (¼ cup)
- (8-inch) flour tortillas
- Ground cumin (½ teaspoon)

Getting ready:
1. Add the chili powder, jalapeño pepper, coriander, scallion, cream cheese, red bell pepper, and cumin to a dish and mix well.
2. Distribute the mixture evenly between the three tortillas, expanding the cheese in a light layer.
3. Fold tortillas the same as a jelly roll; cover them all tightly in the plastic coat.
4. After about an hour, pop them into the freezer.
5. Slice the tortilla rolls and prepare them on a serving plate.

DESSERT

125. Choco-Peanut Protein Bites

What we need:
- 1 cup of peanut butter that does not have extra sugar
- 1 cup of chocolate
- 1 cup protein powder that is flavored (e.g., chocolate)

Getting ready:
1. Place the chocolate in the appliance that cooks.
2. Give it some time to become liquid-like in consistency.
3. Mix the peanut butter and the protein in a mixing bowl.
4. It needs to be slightly sticky, like play dough.
5. Outline the protein combination into balls using your hand.
6. Cook the balls by dipping them in the pot.
7. Maintaining the correct amount of liquid in the chocolate requires that you keep the stove on the whole time.
8. After dipping, the balls should be chilled.

126. Cherry Cake

What we need:
- Pie filling: cherry (20 oz.)
- Butter, unsalted (½ cup)
- Sour cream (1 cup)
- 2 cups of white flour
- Two eggs
- 1 tsp. vanilla
- 1 tsp. baking powder
- Sugar

Getting ready:
1. Preheat your microwave (350°F) and dissolve the butter.
2. Mix the butter, eggs, sour cream, and vanilla in a tiny bowl; combine finely.
3. Toss the flour and baking powder together in a separate basin.
4. Later, combine the two mixtures, folding to mix thoroughly.
5. Grease your pan and pour the batter.
6. Expand the cherry mixture over the batter.
7. Bake them for around 40 minutes.

127. Special Cake

What we need:
- Carob flour (¼ cup)
- Vanilla
- 1½ cups sugar
- 12 egg whites
- Flour (¾ cup)
- Tartar cream (1½ teaspoons)

Getting ready:
1. Heat your oven to 375°F.
2. Add the flour, sugar, and carob flour in a dish; mix well, and place aside.
3. Beat the egg whites and cream of tartar with a whisk for approximately six minutes.
4. The remaining sugar, along with the egg whites, should be mixed together until the sugar is completely dissolved.
5. Combine the flour and vanilla extract in a separate bowl.
6. Spread the mixture on a cake pan.
7. Stream a knife through the mixture to remove all air holes.
8. Bake the cake for approximately 30 minutes.
9. Place the pan on a line stand to chill.

128. Avocado Chocolate Mousse

What we need:
- Three fully ripe avocados, peeled and seeded
- ¼ cup cocoa powder
- ¼ cup almond milk (unsweetened)
- ¼ cup powdered erythritol or your preferred sweetener
- 1 teaspoon of vanilla essence
- A little of salt
- Whipped cream and raspberries for garnish

Getting ready:
1. Place the cocoa powder, ripe avocados, vanilla essence, almond milk, powdered erythritol, and a pinch of salt in the blender.
2. Make sure the mixture is smooth and creamy by blending it well.
3. Taste and adjust the attractiveness if needed by totaling more elements.
4. Remove the chocolate avocado mousse from the serving dishes.
5. Wait at least half an hour for it to freeze before serving.

6. If you'd like, top with whipped cream and some fresh raspberries.

129. Berry Parfait

What we need:
- 1 cup mixed berries like blueberries, strawberries, or raspberries
- 1 cup Greek yogurt (unsweetened)
- ¼ cup chopped nuts
- 1 teaspoon of vanilla essence
- 1 tablespoon powdered erythritol or your preferred sweetener

Getting ready:
1. Take a bowl and combine the Greek yogurt with vanilla essence and powdered erythritol, waiting to be sweetened to your liking.
2. In serving glasses or bowls, coat the Greek yogurt mixture, assorted berries, and chopped nuts.
3. Build up to using all of the ingredients by repeating the layers.
4. Chill the berry parfait in the refrigerator for about 15–20 minutes before serving.
5. Enjoy this fruity and satisfying dessert!

130. Chocolate Peanut Butter Bombs

What we need:
- ½ cup unsweetened peanut butter
- ¼ cup coconut oil, melted
- 2 tablespoons of cocoa powder
- 2 tablespoons powdered erythritol or your preferred sweetener
- ½ teaspoon vanilla essence
- A little of salt

Getting ready:
1. Take a mixing bowl and combine the unsweetened peanut butter, melted coconut oil, unsweetened cocoa powder, powdered erythritol, vanilla essence, and a little salt. Blend until smooth.
2. Use a paper liner to line the inside of a mini-muffin cooker.
3. Ladle the mixture into the muffin cups, filling each about halfway.
4. Freeze for about 20–30 minutes, so that the fat bombs are solid.
5. Store the keto peanut butter chocolate fat bombs in an airtight container in the freezer.
6. Enjoy these sweet and satisfying fat bombs as a treat!

131. Apple Kuchen

What we need:
- Two apples, diced (around 3 cups)
- Granulated sugar (2 cups)
- Two eggs, beaten
- Unsalted butter
- Vanilla essence (2 teaspoons)
- Allspice
- 2 cups of flour
- Ground cinnamon (2 teaspoons)
- Nutmeg
- Soda substitute (1 teaspoon)

Getting ready:
1. Pre-heat your oven.
2. Oil a glassful cooker with butter; set aside.
3. Add the butter and sugar to a dish and combine with a thumb mixer until fluffy.
4. Later, add the vanilla and eggs to the bowl and beat until mixed.
5. Mix the nutmeg, baking soda substitute, cinnamon, flour, and allspice in another bowl; stir well.
6. Add the dry elements and wet elements together and stir well.
7. Mix in the apple and place the combination into the cooker.
8. Cook it in the oven for around one hour so that the cake is brown.
9. Let them cool.

132. Cheese Bites

What we need:

For the cheesecake:
- 7 ounces of softened creamy cheese
- ½ cup powdered erythritol
- 1 teaspoon of pure vanilla essence
- 1 lemon zest
- ½ lemons Sap

For the almond flour crust:
- 5 tablespoons of liquefy butter
- 1 cup of almond flour
- 2 tablespoons of powdered erythritol

Getting ready:
1. Take a dish and mix together softened powdered erythritol, cream cheese, lemon zest, pure vanilla essence, and lemon juice until smooth.
2. In a separate bowl, combine almond flour, powdered erythritol, and melted butter to create the crust mixture.
3. Row a mini-muffin tin with paper liners.
4. Press a tiny amount of the almond flour crust mixture into the bottom of each liner. Transfer the cheesecake filling to the crust using a spoon.
5. Cool it for minimum 2 hours until the cheesecake bites firm up. Serve and enjoy these delightful keto cheesecake bites!

133. Chia Seed Pudding with Berries

What we need:
- 1 cup almond milk
- ¼ cup chia seeds
- ¼ teaspoon vanilla essence
- ½ tablespoon powdered erythritol
- Mixed berries (e.g., strawberries, blueberries, raspberries)
- Sliced almonds for garnish (optional)

Getting ready:
1. Put the chia seeds in a dish and add the unsweetened almond milk, the powdered erythritol, and the pure vanilla extract. Mix well. Combine thoroughly.
2. Place the entire thing in the refrigerator for at least two hours or overnight, shaking it every so often to keep it from clumping.
3. Once the chia seed pudding has thickened, spoon it into serving dishes.
4. Top with mixed berries and sliced almonds for added texture and flavor.
5. Dessert lovers, consider this chia seed pudding with berries—a velvety and healthy choice.

134. Vanilla Coconut Macaroons

What we need:
- 2 cups grated coconut
- ½ cup powdered erythritol
- The white part of 2 eggs
- ½ teaspoon vanilla essence
- A little bit of salt

Getting ready:

1. Prepare your oven by preheating it to 325 degrees Fahrenheit (160 degrees Celsius). Use parchment paper to line a baking sheet.
2. Take a bowl; mix together unsweetened shredded coconut, powdered erythritol, egg whites, pure vanilla essence, and a little salt to finely combine.
3. Drop spoonfuls of the mixture onto the set parchment paper. Make sure the macaroons are lightly golden by baking them for 15-20 minutes.
4. Allow them to chill before serving these delightful vanilla coconut macaroons.

135. Classic Almond Chocolate Cake

What we need:
- ½ cups of almond flour
- Big four eggs
- Sliced almonds are enough for ½ cup.
- 2/3 cups of cocoa powder
- 3/4 cup of granulated erythritol
- ½ cups of grass-fed butter, melted
- 1/4 tablespoon of Dutch-process cocoa, dark
- Baking powder, two tablespoons
- Cup of Heavy Cream, 34 oz.
- Almond essence, pure, one teaspoon
- Sprinkle of salt

Getting ready:
1. Use a spray made from coconut oil to prepare your slow cooker.
2. Put the dry ingredients (flour, salt, baking, protein, erythritol, and cocoa powder) into a big dish.
3. Combine the butter, almond essence, and heavy cream in a separate dish.
4. Combine the liquid with the dry elements by mixing the almonds with a crunch.
5. Put the batter in your pan and up against the lid.
6. If you like a pudding-like dessert, cook it at a low temperature for 2–12 hours; if you prefer a cake-like treat, cook it at a higher temperature for 3–6 hours.
7. Allow 20–30 minutes of cooking time in the off-crock pot before serving.

136. Chocolate Chip Raspberry Muffin Cake

What we need:
- Big four eggs
- One cup of shredded coconut, unsweetened
- ½ of full-fat cream
- ¼ cups of coconut oil liquid
- Almond meal for two cups
- Either ½ cups of stevia or erythritol
- Amount of sugar-free chocolate chips: 13 cups
- 1/4 ounces of Dutch-process cocoa, dark
- grass-fed butter, melted, in a cup
- One cupful of clean raspberries
- Baking soda, two tablespoons
- Sprinkle of salt

Getting ready:
1. Use a spray made from coconut oil to grease your slow cooker.
2. Take all the dry elements into a mixing bowl.
3. Combine eggs, coconut oil, ghee, and cream in another bowl and whisk them all nicely.
4. Toss with the rest of the dry ingredients (coconut included).
5. Blend with some chocolate chips and fresh raspberries.
6. Drop the batter into the pot and close the lid.
7. Putting it in a steamer and leaving it for three hours.
8. Wait until it is cool to remove it with a spatula and serve.

137. Decadent Dark Chocolate Almond Cake

What we need:
- Almond flour, 2 tablespoons
- 1 tablespoon of baking powder
- A dozen of each:
- Cocoa nibs
- Turn in the grains.
- Protein powder made from egg whites or whey, 3 tablespoons
- ¼ t. salt
- 2/3 cup of unsweetened almond milk
- A dozen little eggs
- Vanilla essence ¼ tsp

- Melted butter, 6 tablespoons
- ¼ cup chopped nuts (sugar-free)

Getting ready:
1. Oil or spray a six-quart slow cooker and have it ready.
2. Add the whey protein powder to the sweetener, almond flour, baking powder, salt, and cocoa powder, and blend nicely.
3. Blend the butter, eggs, vanilla, and milk together by folding the ingredients together. Mix with some chips, and serve. Put the batter in the saucepan and cook it for however long you like.
4. Then, after 20 or 30 minutes, remove the heat. Prepare by slicing and serving.

138. Zesty Lemon Custard

What we need:
- 1/4 cup of freshly squeezed lemon juice
- 1 cup of heavy cream
- Zest of one lemon, one tablespoon
- Vanilla essence, 1 teaspoon
- Stevia in liquid form, ½ tablespoons
- A dozen little eggs, white

Getting ready:
1. Blend the egg yolks, lemon sap, and zest, along with the vanilla and stevia.
2. To dish up, divide into four ramekins and fold in the cream.
3. Place the ramekins on a cooling rack and place them inside your steamer. You may make do with a pile of crumpled foil. The ramekins shouldn't be resting directly on the cooker's bottom.
4. Water should be added to the ramekins when it reaches approximately one-third of the way up their sides. Just next to the pot lid.
5. Putting it in a steamer and leaving it for three hours.
6. Take the ramekins out after the time is up and allow them to chill to a normal temperature.
7. Put it in the cooler for a minimum of three hours.
8. Do what you like with the serving!

139. Garlic Basil Cauliflower Cheese Bread

What we need:
- Cauliflower, weighing a total of 1 head
- 2 tablespoons of mozzarella
- A half teaspoon of salt and two whole garlic cloves
- 2 eggs
- 2 teaspoons of finely ground coconut
- To taste black pepper
- Fresh basil

Getting ready:
1. Cauliflower should be chopped.
2. Combine a third of the cheese, flour, pepper, cauliflower, and salt in a mixing basin.
3. Put all of the aforementioned ingredients into the cooker.
4. Include the leftover cheese along with the minced garlic in the dish.
5. Prepare on a high heat for three hours.
6. Basil should be used as a garnish.

140. Chocolate Cake

What we need:
- 1.5 liters of a sweetening agent
- 5 tablespoons of unsweetened cocoa powder to make the chocolate
- 3 eggs
- ½ teaspoon of vanilla essence
- 1 teaspoon baking powder
- 4 ounces of chocolate chips that are sugar-free in composition
- A half a cup of flour that is gluten-free
- A half teaspoon and a half of salt
- A half-cup of butter
- 3 egg yolks
- 0.5 teaspoon liquid stevia, vanilla
- 2 measured cups of boiling water

Getting ready:
1. Mix together 1.25 tablespoons each of flour, cocoa powder, salt, and baking powder.
2. First, in another bowl, thoroughly combine the egg whites, vanilla essence, melted butter, and stevia.

3. Put everything that has been listed above into the slow cooker. Put chocolate chunks in the saucer.
4. Mix the boiling water with the rest of the flour in a mixing bowl.
5. Cook on low heat for three hours.

141. Chocolate Almond Brownies

What we need:
- 1 standard cup of ground almonds
- 2 teaspoons of almond flour, half a cup, and a half of cocoa powder
- 1.5 tablespoons of the powdered baking ingredient
- Three hen's eggs
- 0.66 ml of milk made from almonds
- 0.33 grams of sugar-free chocolate chips, including chips
- A half-cup of swerve
- 3 tablespoons each of whey protein isolate, protein powder, and unflavored
- 0.25 grams of salt in a teaspoon
- There should be 6 tablespoons of butter.
- A vanilla essence equivalent to 0.75 tablespoons

Getting ready:
1. Sweetener, protein powder, salt, almond flour, cocoa powder, and baking powder should be mixed together in a dish with a whisk.
2. Blend in the eggs, butter, vanilla essence, and egg yolks before adding the almond milk.
3. The cooker is where you should put everything.
4. Bake on steam for two hours.
5. Wait thirty minutes for it to cool off.

142. Cheesecake

What we need:

Crust:
- A couple of teaspoons' worth of butter
- Stevia to taste
- 1 ounce (or cup) of pecans
- 1 egg

Filling:
- Cream cheese, measuring 16 ounces in volume
- One and a half milligrams of stevia
- 4 tablespoons of full-fat whipping cream

- Two eggs
- One teaspoon of the essence of vanilla bean

Getting ready:
1. You will need to grind the nuts and then muddle them in with the rest of the elements for the crust.
2. In the slow cooker, mold into a pie crust.
3. Combine the ingredients for the filling.
4. Place the crust on top.
5. Include one cup of water in the mix.
6. Prepare on a high heat for two hours.
7. Just give it some time.

143. Carrot Cake Delight

What we need:

Cake:
- 5 cups of ground almonds and 0.5 cups of ground coconut
- A half teaspoon of vanilla essence
- ¼ of a cup of walnuts
- Two tablespoons of the powdered baking ingredient
- 25 milligrams of ground cloves
- 2 measuring cups of carrots
- A quarter of a cup of coconut oil
- 25 cups of unflavored whey protein powder, which is a protein powder.
- One and a half milligrams of cinnamon
- 25 grams of salt in a teaspoon
- 4 eggs
- Almond milk, to the extent of three tablespoons

Frosting:
- Cheese cream measuring 6 ounces in volume
- 75 milligrams of vanilla essence
- 5 cups of stevia
- A half cup of heavy cream

Getting ready:

Cake:
1. Apply oil to the inside of the cooker.
2. Mix all the following elements in a dish: flour, coconut, protein, cinnamon, salt, sweetener, nuts, baking powder, and cloves.

3. After that, stir in the eggs, almond milk, carrots, coconut oil, and vanilla essence.
4. Combine each of the constituent parts well.
5. Pour into the inside of the cooker.
6. Cook on low heat for three hours.
7. Just give it some time.

Frosting:
1. Combine the sweetener and cheese cream in a thorough mixing.
2. Combine the vanilla with the cream.
3. Blend to a silky smoothness.
4. Spread over the cooled cake.

144. Energy Bites

What we need:
- 1 cup of peanut butter that does not have extra sugar
- 1 cup of chocolate
- 1 cup protein powder that is flavored (e.g., chocolate)

Getting ready:
1. Place the chocolate in the appliance that cooks.
2. Give it some time to become liquid-like in consistency.
3. Mix the peanut butter and the protein in a mixing bowl.
4. It needs to be slightly sticky, like play dough.
5. Outline the protein combination into balls using your hand.
6. Cook the balls by dipping them in the pot.
7. Maintaining the correct amount of liquid in the chocolate requires that you keep the stove on the whole time.
8. After dipping, the balls should be chilled.

30-Day Meal Plan

Week 1

Day 1:
- **Breakfast:** Blueberry-Banana Smoothie
- **Lunch:** Grilled Chicken and Avocado Salad
- **Dinner:** Classic Pot Roast
- **Snack:** Caprese Skewers with Balsamic Glaze

Day 2:
- **Breakfast:** Omelet
- **Lunch:** Herb Pesto Pork Chops
- **Dinner:** Baked Salmon with Lemon-Dill Sauce
- **Snack:** Greek Yogurt with Berries and Almonds

Day 3:
- **Breakfast:** Almond-Cranberry Cereal Bar
- **Lunch:** Beef Stir-up
- **Dinner:** Eggplant Lasagna
- **Snack:** Parmesan Zucchini Crisps

Day 4:
- **Breakfast:** Chewy Date-Apple Bars
- **Lunch:** Adobo Chicken
- **Dinner:** Lemon, Garlic, Shrimp, and Asparagus
- **Snack:** Smoked Salmon with Cucumber

Day 5:
- **Breakfast:** Fried Eggs with Spinach and Mushrooms
- **Lunch:** Beef Bread
- **Dinner:** Grilled Portobello Mushrooms with Spinach and Feta
- **Snack:** Almond and Coconut Energy Bites

Day 6:
- **Breakfast:** Greek Yogurt with Berry Bliss
- **Lunch:** Persian Chicken
- **Dinner:** Spaghetti Squash with Pesto and Cherry Tomatoes
- **Snack:** Spicy Roasted Chickpeas

Day 7:
- **Breakfast:** Avocado and Egg Breakfast Delight
- **Lunch:** Special Noodles
- **Dinner:** Baked Chicken Thighs with Garlic and Herbs
- **Snack:** Mini Bell Pepper Nachos

Week 2

Day 8:
- **Breakfast:** Spinach and Mushroom Frittata
- **Lunch:** Fried Rice with Cauliflower
- **Dinner:** Zoodles with Meatballs in an Italian Sauce
- **Snack:** Cauliflower Buffalo Bites

Day 9:
- **Breakfast:** Smoked Salmon and Cheese Roll
- **Lunch:** Cauliflower and Broccoli Soup
- **Dinner:** Curried Cauliflower Soup
- **Snack:** Crispy Cheese

Day 10:
- **Breakfast:** Green Smoothie
- **Lunch:** Stuffed Vegetables with Mushroom
- **Dinner:** Shrimp Gravy
- **Snack:** Meatballs

Day 11:
- **Breakfast:** Berry Crumble Pudding
- **Lunch:** Quiche Lorraine
- **Dinner:** Cauliflower Rice and Luau Pork
- **Snack:** Sweet and Spicy Shrimp

Day 12:
- **Breakfast:** Chewy Date-Apple Bars
- **Lunch:** Chicken Gyros
- **Dinner:** Roasted-Beef Stew
- **Snack:** Cheesy Spaghetti Squash

Day 13:
- **Breakfast:** Breakfast Meatloaf
- **Lunch:** Chicken Satay
- **Dinner:** Chicken Noodle Soup
- **Snack:** Prosciutto-Garlic Green Beans

Day 14:

- **Breakfast:** Mixed Veggie Omelet
- **Lunch:** Pork Chops
- **Dinner:** Baked Cod with Lemon and Herbs
- **Snack:** Fresh Veggies with Herbs

Week 3

Day 15:
- **Breakfast:** Cheesy Eggs, Bacon, and Cauliflower Hash
- **Lunch:** Chicken Loaf
- **Dinner:** Lemon Herb Grilled Chicken Breast
- **Snack:** Veggie Stir-Fry

Day 16:
- **Breakfast:** Poached Salmon
- **Lunch:** Granola and Grilled Peaches
- **Dinner:** Spicy Cauliflower Rice with Ground Turkey
- **Snack:** Pizza Casserole

Day 17:
- **Breakfast:** Cottage Cheese with Nut Medley
- **Lunch:** Zesty Mediterranean Chicken Thighs
- **Dinner:** Grilled Chicken and Vegetable Stir-Fry
- **Snack:** Sweet and Spicy Thai Pizza

Day 18:
- **Breakfast:** Vegetable Korma
- **Lunch:** Beef Bourguignon
- **Dinner:** Grilled Cilantro Lime Chicken
- **Snack:** Pancakes

Day 19:
- **Breakfast:** Zucchini Soup
- **Lunch:** Classic Pot Roast
- **Dinner:** Lamb with Asparagus
- **Snack:** Twist Pizza

Day 20:
- **Breakfast:** Grilled Citrus Halibut
- **Lunch:** Paneer Curry with Stuffed Potatoes
- **Dinner:** Zoodles with Meatballs in an Italian Sauce
- **Snack:** Diavola Pizza

Day 21:
- **Breakfast:** Special Vegetable Stock

- **Lunch:** Different Chicken Curry
- **Dinner:** Shrimp Thermion
- **Snack:** Vegan Pizza

Week 4

Day 22:
- **Breakfast:** Cappuccino Chocolate Chip
- **Lunch:** Rice with Lentil Curry
- **Dinner:** Roasted Beef Stew
- **Snack:** Grilled Sandwich

Day 23:
- **Breakfast:** Blueberry-Banana Smoothie
- **Lunch:** Baked Egg
- **Dinner:** Soup with Chicken and Noodles
- **Snack:** Mini Burger Sliders

Day 24:
- **Breakfast:** Gumbo with Seafood
- **Lunch:** Tuna and Avocado Salad
- **Dinner:** Beef in a Stir-Fry
- **Snack:** Portobello Mushroom Burger Bites

Day 25:
- **Breakfast:** Breakfast Meatloaf
- **Lunch:** Grilled Shrimp and Vegetable Skewers
- **Dinner:** Walleye Simmered in Basil Cream
- **Snack:** Tacos

Day 26:
- **Breakfast:** Turkey Casserole
- **Lunch:** Lamb and Pork Seasoning
- **Dinner:** Cheesy Tuna Casserole
- **Snack:** Chicken and Vegetable Kabobs

Day 27:
- **Breakfast:** Waffle Sandwich
- **Lunch:** Simple Chicken Gravy
- **Dinner:** Ginger Beef Salad
- **Snack:** Roasted Pepper with Chicken

Day 28:
- **Breakfast:** Bagel Sandwich
- **Lunch:** Crab Cakes with Lime Salsa

- **Dinner:** French Onion Soup
- **Snack:** Antojitos

Day 29:
- **Breakfast:** Almond-Cranberry Cereal Bar
- **Lunch:** Deviled Egg with Pickled Jalapenos
- **Dinner:** Traditional Chicken-Vegetable Soup
- **Snack:** Guacamole-Stuffed Cucumber Bites

Day 30:
- **Breakfast:** Cherry Scones
- **Lunch:** Cobbler Topped with Chicken Gravy
- **Dinner:** Grilled Chicken and Vegetable Stir-Fry
- **Snack:** Caprese Skewers with Balsamic Glaze

CONCLUSION

Embarking on a culinary journey to manage insulin resistance can be both fulfilling and enjoyable. This cookbook offers a variety of delicious and nutritious recipes designed to support your health goals while satisfying your taste buds. Every meal, from filling breakfasts to satiating feasts, is designed to support holistic health and help you keep your blood sugar levels in check.

Including these meals in your regular routine might change the way you feel about eating. The focus on whole, unprocessed ingredients ensures you receive essential nutrients while avoiding unnecessary sugars and unhealthy fats. By following these recipes, you can enjoy the benefits of a diet that supports insulin sensitivity and reduces the risk of related health issues.

Adopting an insulin resistance diet might require a major adjustment to one's way of life, but it can also have a large positive impact on one's health with proper preparation and dedication. Take charge of your insulin resistance and strive toward a healthy future by emphasizing portion management, hydration, a balanced diet, and frequent exercise.

Recall that consistency is essential. Your health may significantly improve with minor, long-lasting modifications to your dietary habits. This cookbook is not just a collection of recipes but a tool to empower you on your journey to better health. As you explore these meals, you'll discover that managing insulin resistance doesn't mean compromising on flavor or enjoyment.

We appreciate you using this cookbook as a starting point. May it inspire you to cook with creativity and confidence, nourishing your body and embracing a healthier lifestyle?

Made in United States
North Haven, CT
04 December 2024